DATE DUE

~~JV 24~~			
~~NO 20 97~~			
~~AP 20 '98~~			
~~NO 30 98~~			
~~JE 11 '00~~			
~~AG 5 03~~			
~~AP 1 '05~~			

DEMCO 38-296

THE INDESTRUCTIBLE BOOK

THE INDESTRUCTIBLE BOOK

THE BIBLE, ITS TRANSLATORS, AND THEIR SACRIFICES

W. Kenneth Connolly

Baker Books

A Division of Baker Book House Co
Grand Rapids, Michigan 49516

Riverside Community College
Library
4800 Magnolia Avenue
Riverside, California 92506

© 1996 W. Kenneth Connolly

BS 445 .C66 1996

Connolly, W. Kenneth, 1927-

The indestructible Book

only exception is brief quotations in
printed reviews.

**Library of Congress
Cataloging-in-Publication Data**
Connolly, W. Kenneth, 1927–
    The indestructible Book / W. Kenneth
Connolly.
        p.   cm.
    Includes index.
    ISBN 0–8010–1126–4
    1. Bible—History.   2. Bible.
English—Versions.   I. Title.
BS445.C66   1996
220'.09—dc20   98–8391
                                           CIP

Designed by Three's Company

Worldwide coedition organised and
produced by Angus Hudson Ltd,
Concorde House, Grenville Place,
Mill Hill, London NW7 3SA, England
Tel: +44 181 959 3668
Fax: +44 181 959 3678

Printed in Hong Kong

Picture acknowledgements

British & Foreign Bible Society: p. 184
British Library: pp. 45, 56 (bottom), 77, 160,
167
Chris Bueno: pp. 12, 15, 55, 56 (top right),
89, 90, 164, 170, 171, 175
Tim Dowley: pp. 12, 13, 18, 19, 20, 23, 26,
31, 35, 46, 61, 65 (top), 126
Mary Evans Picture Library: pp. 32, 33, 41,
42, 48, 51, 53, 56 (top), 64, 65 (bottom), 81
(top), 87, 91, 157, 172, 173
Mansell Collection: 16, 17, 34, 37, 39, 47, 54
(top), 55, 59, 63, 71, 81 (bottom), 83, 85, 88,
95, 96, 97, 99, 103, 106, 107, 113, 115, 122,
123, 124, 128, 135, 146, 147, 151, 153, 169
Tony Morris: Title page, contents page, p.
145
National Portrait Gallery, London: pp. 109,
111, 117, 119, 129, 139, 161, 165, 183, 187,
189
John Rylands Library: p. 44
Peter Wyart: pp. 8, 10, 11, 14, 21, 25, 36, 52,
54 (bottom), 73, 75, 77, 84, 105, 110, 127,
133, 141, 143, 177, 188

Contents

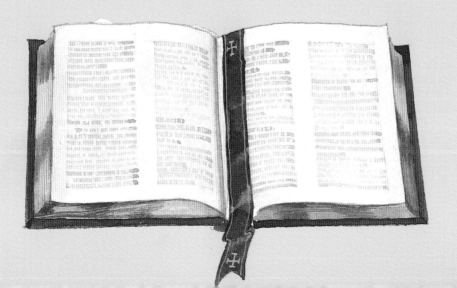

1. A Book in the Making

A unique volume

The Bible is the most remarkable piece of literature this world has ever seen. It has outsold every other publication, it has been translated into more languages than any other, and has become part of the fabric of society in the English-speaking world. You will find it in someone's hands almost every time you see a christening, a wedding or a funeral; and the authorities make people swear by it in almost every Western law court.

Humanly speaking, it took more than 1,500 years to compile the Bible. About forty authors contributed, and they wrote primarily in Greek and Hebrew, with occasional Aramaic. Some used poetry, others wrote history, and yet others biography. Some were kings, but others peasants; some were warriors and others priests; some were devoted patriots, and others members of an outlawed underground organization. What they produced has come to us in two Testaments, with their 66 books, broken into 1,189 chapters and 31,173 verses.

Some people were so committed to the belief that this is God's book that they were even willing to die for that proposition. And strangely, others have been willing to put them to death. The bitterness and resentment against this book are difficult to explain. The cruelest of instruments have been used in an effort to prevent its propagation. Body racks, tongue pinchers, thumb screws, iron boots and whipping trees have all been used in attempts to turn supporters against the Bible. Such supporters have been hung, drawn and quartered; they have been burned, boiled and beheaded. Even in the twentieth century in some countries men and women have been imprisoned and tortured for reading this forbidden book.

How are we to classify the Bible? Each of us must make up our own mind about this extraordinary book.

One inescapable conclusion is that this book is Christ-centred.

The Old Testament opens like an old weather-beaten chart. People who foreshadow Christ walk across its pages: people such as Adam, Melchizedek, Joseph, Moses and David.

Bethlehem—the little town in the Judean hills which has become central to the Christian story.

Similarly, structures and rituals foreshadow Christ. Unfamiliar structures were erected, such as the Tabernacle, its altar protected by a veil; or a strange ship, called the Ark, which weathered the world's worst storm. Equally strange rituals were observed. The Passover required a slaughtered lamb, the Day of Atonement needed an exiled goat, a leper's cleansing was celebrated with the killing of two birds. Then there were typical offices like those of the prophet, the priest and the king, all roles later ascribed to Jesus.

When all these blurry pictures come into focus, the entire Old Testament can be seen as a picture of the Jewish Messiah. To the writers of the New Testament, this Jewish Messiah was none other than Jesus of Nazareth. To the leaders of the synagogues, this Nazarene was but the son of a carpenter, and therefore a fraud. They did not deny His supernatural abilities, but they concluded that His miracles were actually empowered by Satan. To the Roman government, He could have posed a serious threat. He accepted the title of "king," as an heir to the throne of Israel's great king David. His talk about the building of a kingdom, even misunderstood by some of His disciples, seemed to threaten the relative peace of the worldwide Roman empire.

The opening pages of the New Testament put a spotlight on this person of Christ. Jesus taught that the Jewish scriptures were but a foreword, written to prepare for His coming. Jesus said, "Search the scriptures, for in them ye think ye have eternal life: and they are they which testify of me" (John 5:39). Even the apostles said, "To him give all the prophets witness" (Acts 10:43).

Dr. Luke first wrote his Gospel of the life of Christ, then wrote the book of Acts. While it might be assumed that his Acts was merely a postscript to his Gospel, he carefully defined it otherwise: "The former treatise have I made . . . of all that Jesus began to do and teach, until the day in which he was taken up" (Acts 1:1). Luke was suggesting that Jesus invaded all subsequent history. He implied that the history of the early church, recorded in the book of Acts, was but the continuation of the work and teaching of Jesus.

This New Testament teaching about Christ's entrance into the world became so commonly accepted that even the calendars were changed. All previous history was now dated "before Christ" (BC), and all subsequent history dated *Anno Domini* (AD), a Latin description meaning "in the year of the Lord."

To find out more about the significance of Jesus, let us go to Bethlehem.

This book is alive

Bethlehem is a sleepy little town whose history goes all the way back to Genesis. It has been associated with both sadness and gladness. It was

here that Abraham's grandson Jacob buried his beloved wife Rachel. The prophet Jeremiah later said that if you sit quietly by her grave, you could still hear her weeping for her children. Perhaps most infamous of all the tragic events took place after Herod the king called in his wise men to instruct him where the Messiah was to be born. They quoted Micah: "But thou, Bethlehem Ephratah, though thou be little among the thousands of Judah, yet out of thee shall he come forth unto me that is to be ruler in Israel . . ." (Micah 5:2). Herod "slew all the children that were in Bethlehem, and in all the coasts thereof, from two years old and under" (Matthew 2:16).

But tragedies gave place to triumphs. Very happy memories are also associated with this town of Bethlehem. It was on these hills that the courtship between Ruth and Boaz matured (Ruth chapters 2–4). An entire book of the Bible is given over to telling their story. And it was to these hills that the prophet Samuel came to find their great grandson, a shepherd boy named David. He was tending his sheep on these hills when Samuel anointed him to be the next king of Israel. That boy loved this place so dearly that, when it was taken by the Philistines, he sighed:

The Bethlehem skyline is punctuated by church towers and minarets.

"Oh that one would give me drink of the water of the well of Bethlehem, which is by the gate!" (2 Samuel 23:15). Great warriors risked their lives to bring that refreshing drink to David, and he poured it out as a thank-offering unto the Lord.

Later, the most stupendous event of Christian history happened here. It was here that Jesus Christ was born. He is not simply a picture on a Christmas card; He is not a fairy-tale character in a children's story book. There is no question that he lived; contemporary Jewish and secular historians refer to His miracles, His death, and His enormous influence.

Jesus made some fantastic claims about Himself. He claimed to be the Son of God. He said that He was sent by the Father to lead humanity into salvation. He also claimed that he was "the way, the truth, and the life," and that no man could come to the Father except through Him (John 14:6). Confucius, Buddha, and even Muhammad never made such claims. But Jesus' greatest prediction related to His sacrificial death, to be followed by a resurrection from the dead, three days later.

The site in the Church of the Nativity, Bethlehem, that is revered as the place where Jesus was born.

Gordon's Calvary, Jerusalem, proposed by General Gordon as the site of Golgotha—the "Place of the Skull"—since it resembled a human skull.

To the Jewish religious leaders, Jesus' claims were preposterous, in fact blasphemous; so one bitter morning He was taken to the rock shaped like a skull and nailed to a "tree," in crucifixion. Many students of the Bible believe they can identify the actual location of that crucifixion. But the hilltop did not end His story. In the same rock formation there was a hewn tomb, which many historians believe was the place where they laid His lifeless body. To make sure there was no tampering, an enormous stone was rolled against the mouth of the tomb. It was sealed and soldiers were posted to guard it. Early the following Sunday, women came to embalm His body, only to find the stone rolled away. Although the wrappings were still there, His body was missing.

Every conceivable explanation has been put forward to discredit the possibility of a resurrection. The disciples were accused of "stealing" the body, though no explanation was given as to how they could have accomplished this, nor was a warrant ever issued for their arrest. The guards confessed to falling asleep, though no disciplinary measures were ever taken against them. How could a sleeping guard know what actually happened?

To the writers of the New Testament, and Christians throughout history, Jesus was not merely a man. They believed His resurrection proved that He was the incarnation of God, the Messiah, the Savior of humankind. So the apostle Paul wrote to the church at Corinth arguing that if Christ be not risen from the dead, preaching is useless, faith is futile and we are still in our sins (1 Corinthians 15:14–17). To all true believers, His resurrection is cardinal, pivotal, and fundamental.

The Jewish religious leaders and the Roman officials considered Jesus' death to be the closing of an unpleasant chapter in the brief tale of an upstart religious sect. In fact it proved to be the opening chapter in

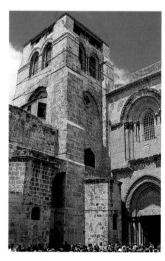

The Church of the Holy Sepulchre, Jerusalem, by strong tradition the site of Jesus' crucifixion and burial.

the story of a mighty, and sometimes militant, force known as the Christian church. This new movement infiltrated the fabric of Rome's imperial power. The church, in fact, forced Rome, first, to recognize her; later, to join with her; and still later, to submit to her.

To understand the impact of this event, we must first analyze the age in which the first Christians lived. That will, in turn, require an understanding of the years preceding the coming of the New Testament. The Jews had a Bible which Jesus knew thoroughly, quoted frequently, and about which He argued continuously with the religious leaders of His day. What was the Bible which Jesus and His disciples knew?

The making of the Old Testament

If there is one word which you need to put into your vocabulary when thinking about the origins of the Bible, it is the word "canon." This word refers to the books which together compose Holy Scripture. They were communicated to us by God, through special men, and became authoritative, distinct from all other writings. The Jewish canon, which is limited to the Old Testament, was publicly acknowledged long before the birth of Christ, but the official closing of the canon took place in AD 100 at a rabbinical assembly in Jamnia, thirteen miles south of modern Tel Aviv. None of the books that were written between the end of our Old Testament and the beginning of the New Testament—known as the Apocrypha—were considered by the Jews to be inspired.

The Garden Tomb, just outside the Damascus Gate, Jerusalem —a haven of peace, and offering an example of a rock-hewn tomb.

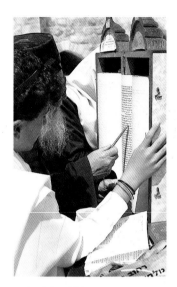

A Jewish rabbi points to a scroll of the Law, or Torah, at the Western Wall, Jerusalem.

But any Jewish religious scholar would explain to you that the canon was not decided by a single act of man, but done "gradually from God." In the days of Jesus, the Scriptures consisted of the Law, or Torah; followed by the Prophets; and then the *"Hagiographa,"* or the Writings. This was the division that Jesus used in Luke 24:44.

The Old Testament was first written in Hebrew. The Hebrew language did not distinguish between capital and small letters. It had no vowels or punctuation marks, and writing was from right to left. There were 22 letters in the Hebrew alphabet, and 22 books in the Jewish Bible. It contained, nevertheless, the same material that we have in the 39 books of our Old Testament. We divide First and Second Samuel, Kings and Chronicles, while the Jews did not. Jeremiah's Lamentations they considered one with his prophecy, and so on.

How did the Old Testament come together? In Exodus 24:4 we read: "And Moses wrote all the words of the Lord." These were placed "in the side of the Ark of the Covenant," according to Deuteronomy 31:26. Joshua later added to them; and still later Samuel "told the people the manner of the kingdom, and wrote it in a book, and laid it up before the Lord" (1 Samuel 10:25). Much later "Hilkiah the high priest said unto Shaphan the scribe, I have found the book of the law in the house of the Lord . . ." (2 Kings 22:8). These passages show that the records gradually grew, and were safely protected.

It was long assumed that the claims of Moses to have written down the law were groundless, because nobody was supposed to have known anything about the art of writing until a much later period. However, at the end of the last century, something happened which helped scholars to change their minds about the origin of writing. In 1887 an Egyptian peasant woman was walking among the ruins of Tel el-Amarna looking for something to sell when her foot hit a hard object in the sand: it was a piece of hardened clay, covered with unusual markings. She invited a friend to help her dig, and they did not give up until they had a bag full of these baked clay tablets.

What she had stumbled upon was the Egyptian Foreign Office archive of that ancient period. We now know that long before the days of Moses, ambassadors had an active postal service, regularly reporting affairs from distant regions of Palestine. Not only would Moses have known how to write, 1,500 years before Christ, but some who study the science of paleography believe that the book of Job perhaps predates Moses by more than 400 years.

In 586 BC a devastating event occurred: Jerusalem was captured by the Babylonians. The Temple was looted and then destroyed by fire, and hundreds of prisoners were taken off to be settled in faraway Babylon. There they met in small groups, probably in each other's houses, for worship and instruction. It is thought that this marked the beginning of the synagogue movement—the word "synagogue" means "meeting

Jews at the Western Wall (or Wailing Wall), Jerusalem, unroll a scroll of the Law, or Torah.

together." In later years small buildings were built in any town where there was a community of Jews. These were also called "synagogues," and served as community center, town hall, school, law court, and, above all, chapel.

When the majority of Jewish captives returned to Palestine from Babylon, about seventy years later, tradition holds that Ezra collected together the books of the Old Testament which had been miraculously preserved through the turmoil of the Exile.

From the earliest times careful and exact copies of the holy writings had been made by Jewish scholars called "scribes." But after the Exile the role of scribe took on an added importance. Scribes were also priests, and they had the great responsibility of preserving, copying and interpreting the Law. When we meet them in the New Testament, we find that these scribes actively opposed the ministry of Jesus. But this much must be said to their credit: they were fastidious. They regulated their profession as writers as follows:

1. They could use only clean animal skins, both to write on, and even to bind manuscripts.

2. Each column of writing could have no less than forty-eight, and no more than sixty lines.

3. The ink must be black, and of a special recipe.

4. They must "verbalize" each word aloud while they were writing.

5. They must wipe the pen, and wash their entire bodies, before writing the word "Jehovah," every time they wrote it.

6. There must be a "review" within thirty days, and if as many as three pages required correction, the entire document had to be redone.

7. The letters, words and paragraphs had to be counted, and the document became invalid if two letters touched each other. The middle paragraph, word and letter must correspond to those of the original document.

8. All old and worn documents had to be "buried" with ceremonial pomp. (This is why we have none of the original documents today.)

9. The documents could be stored only in sacred places.

10. As no document containing God's Word could be destroyed, they were stored, or buried, in a *genizah*, a Hebrew term meaning "hiding place." These were usually kept in a synagogue, or sometimes in a Jewish cemetery.

The Greeks have a word for it

The prophet Isaiah, looking forward to the time when the Messiah would come, said that He would be "as a root out of a dry ground" (Isaiah 53:2). The "dry ground" referred to was the corrupt character of the age into which the Messiah was to come. The Apostle Paul, looking back at the timing of Jesus' entrance into the world, stated: "When the fullness of the time was come, God sent forth his Son" (Galatians 4:4). Jesus was aware of the timing of His arrival. He said: "The time is fulfilled, and the kingdom of God is at hand" (Mark 1:15).

The celebrated Greek thinker and debater, Socrates.

Both the Greeks and the Romans played a significant role in preparing the world for the entrance of Jesus Christ. When Alexander the Great conquered the world, around 330 BC, he brought the Greek way of life to the east, and with it the thinking of the great Greek philosophers. The world was challenged by the questions of Socrates, Plato and Aristotle, who mentally probed the unknown spirit world. They taught people how to ask questions which provoked them to think; but they could not supply the answers to those questions. They succeeded in putting basic problems into focus, but left a world waiting for someone to come who could provide authoritative answers.

The second major Greek contribution was to provide the world with a single language, known as *koine*, or "common Greek." By the time Alexander died, in 323 BC, the world had become bilingual, and Greek was the second language everybody used. This becomes important for our story of the Bible.

Though the origins of the Greek translation of the Old Testament are veiled in romance and conjecture, the most common version is as follows. Around the year 285 BC, Demetrius of Phalerum was custodian of a world-famous library in Alexandria. Many Jews were living in Egypt, so Demetrius asked King Ptolemy Philadelphus if he could arrange to have a Greek translation of the Jewish Law made for the library.

As a goodwill gesture, the king released 100,000 Jewish slaves, and sent an embassy with rich presents to Eleazar, the high priest in Jerusalem, requesting six able scholars from each of the twelve tribes, totaling seventy-two men, to undertake this task. The scholars were honorably received at the court of Alexandria, and taken to the island of Pharos, so they might work silently and undisturbed. It is reputed that they lived in seventy-two cells, finished their task of translating the Torah in seventy-two days, and were in total agreement over the results of their labour. Because of the number of scholars, this work became known as the Septuagint, the Greek word for "seventy."

I have two important observations about this scholarly work. The seventy-two men apparently continued their translation until they had finished the entire Old Testament canon; then they appended the Apocryphal writings. Jerome, and other early Church Fathers who translated the Bible into Latin, worked from the Septuagint version of the Old Testament—and therefore included the Apocryphal writings. Roman Catholic Bibles were based on these Latin translations, and consequently Roman Catholics accept the inspiration of the Apocrypha. Until the sixteenth century the Eastern churches used the Apocryphal writings. After Luther opposed the Council of Trent, which included the Apocrypha in the canon, Protestants increasingly removed the Apocrypha from the canon, but allowed it for private edification.

Secondly, the influence of the Septuagint was enormous. In the intertestamental period, persecution dispersed the Jews into "every nation under heaven," as Luke puts it in Acts. Jews spoke every known language, and many did not understand the old Hebrew of their Bible. However, everyone knew Greek. So the Septuagint met a very great need, providing the books of Moses for Jews scattered around the world. In fact, it became *the* Bible. It was this book that the apostles referred to as the Word of God.

Plato, Socrates' pupil, and author of *The Republic*.

The beginnings of the New Testament

If we were to take the first century, and analyze it according to how God's truth was communicated, we might divide it as follows:

During the period until AD 30 Jesus was living on earth, so we could call it the time of *living truth*. Jesus was the center of authority. He never wrote a book, He simply said: "Learn of Me," "I am the truth" (Matthew 11:29; John 14:6). He placed Himself in the gravitational center of the spiritual universe and said: "Come unto me, all ye that labor" (Matthew 11:28). It was Christ, and not a creed, which was important.

Nazareth, Jesus' home town, dominated today by the huge Basilica of the Annunciation.

A second period, until AD 50, might be called the time of *oral tradition*. Following Jesus' death, accounts of His words and deeds were passed on by word of mouth.

The final period, from AD 50 onwards, is the time of *written communication*. The apostles could not be everywhere, and they often taught new churches by writing letters. Some of those letters form part of our New Testament.

At this point in our story, we are interested in the days in which Jesus lived, when His life, His actions and His words became the embodiment of truth.

Jesus grew up in the market town of Nazareth. Like all Jewish boys, each morning He went to school in the synagogue, where His only textbook was the Bible. From the age of twelve to about thirty, He probably worked in Nazareth, at Joseph's carpenter's bench. He returned to Nazareth after His baptism, and in the synagogue there He outlined His intended ministry. The people of Nazareth were outraged by His words. They rejected Him and took Him to the edge of a cliff, intending to throw Him over and end His life.

Later Jesus came to the shores of Galilee and made the ancient town of Capernaum the center of His public ministry. He only went to Jerusalem for the great religious festivals.

Lake Galilee is 685 feet below sea-level, about 6 miles wide, 16 miles long, and approximately 130 feet at its maximum depth. Its water provided work for hundreds of fishermen in the many busy fishing villages along its shores. Of the thirty-six miracles which are recorded in the Gospels, nineteen were performed in and around this lake. It was down by the water's edge that Peter caught a fish with a coin in its mouth. On the hillside overlooking the north-east shore of the lake, Jesus preached His famous Sermon on the Mount. In this area, too, He fed 5,000 "men, beside women and children" (Matthew 14:21). A little to the south you can see the steep slope and caves which may be where He calmed the man with a "legion" of demons mastering him (Mark 5). Of the twelve men Jesus selected to become His apostles, eleven came from this region. Only one came from the area of Judea, and he proved to be a traitor and a bitter disappointment.

It was on the surface of this lake that Jesus walked; and, on another occasion, stood up in the prow of a ship and commanded the angry, turbulent waves to lie at peace.

Because Lake Galilee was where Jesus spent most of His ministry, this was where the seeds were sown that would flower as the New Testament. Jesus taught in parables; but examine their teaching. Every truth preached by Paul had been previously planted as a seedling in the parables of Jesus. Look at His miracles. They were "parables in action." They showed that He was Lord over death, disease and demons. These conditions express the general human malady. Death is our spiritual condition; leprosy our defilement by sin; blindness our indifference to spiritual realities; and fever shows us the contagious and restless nature of sin.

Fishing boats moored on Lake Galilee.

For three and a half years Jesus lived with His disciples, ate with them, walked and rested with them. He guided them through long journeys, tedious pressures and restless nights. By words and actions He followed the instructions of Isaiah, and taught them: "precept must be upon precept; line upon line; here a little, and there a little" (Isaiah 28:10). Before He left them, He even promised them that He would send them "another Comforter," who would "bring all things to your remembrance" (John 14:16, 26).

While Paul wrote to the Gentile Christians, Peter wrote to the Hebrew Christians. They were scattered throughout the Roman provinces of Pontus, Galatia, Cappadocia, Asia and Bithynia (1 Peter 1:1), after severe persecution for which they needed the strongest encouragement. Though Peter fades from the pages of Acts after the first twelve chapters, he was faithful to the end of his days. Tradition has it that he died in Rome, crucified upside down because he felt he was unworthy to die upright as his Master had died.

John, the youngest of the apostles, outlived them all. He wrote three letters which inspired holy living, and a Gospel which highlighted themes which the other three writers had omitted. His visionary work, the book of Revelation, was written while he was an exile on the isle of Patmos. John lifted the veil and allowed us to look into the future "Day of the Lord."

By the end of the first century, the foundation for the New Testament was laid. For the next stage, we must turn to Rome.

The Roman theater at Caesarea Maritima—Caesarea-on-Sea— built by Herod the Great and named to honor Caesar.

Remains of the Roman piles and pillars from the harbor at Caesarea.

The Roman contribution

The beautiful marble seaport of Caesarea Maritima stood on the Mediterranean coast, sixty-five miles by road from Jerusalem. It was a new town, built by Herod the Great on the site of a Phoenician fort which Caesar had captured in 22 BC. Engineers constructed a magnificent semi-circular artificial harbor which could accommodate 300 ships. Herod also built an amphitheater, a hippodrome, and amazing aqueducts to channel water to the city from underground springs some distance away. Herod honored Caesar by naming the city for him, and the Romans quickly made it their administrative center.

The succeeding king, Herod Agrippa, often used Caesarea as his capital. It was here, during a time of political unrest, that one day he dressed himself in royal apparel and gave an oration which so overpowered his audience that, according to Luke, they shouted: "It is the voice of a god, and not of a man" (Acts 12:22). But, Luke adds, because Herod did not ascribe credit to God, he fell to the floor and was eaten by intestinal roundworms before his adoring audience (Acts 12:21–23).

In AD 66, the Jews rebelled against the Romans, and were finally crushed four years later. Jerusalem was razed to the ground, and it has been claimed that more than one million people may have been put to death. Many were taken to Caesarea's amphitheater, where they were killed for sport.

Yet Rome played a very important role in preparing the way for the expansion of the early church. The first major contribution was in administrative law. Roman law had been developing ever since the "Twelve Tablets" of 450 BC, which classified the law code in order to

An entrance to the Roman amphitheater at Caesarea Maritima.

clarify the rights of its citizens. Roman law eventually became the foundation for English law, which in turn became the basis for the legal systems of the United States, Canada, Australia, South Africa and most other English speaking countries.

The second major Roman contribution came from their skill as engineers and builders. Whereas the Greeks broke down barriers created by language, the Romans were concerned to eradicate geographical boundaries. They built roads and bridges to make it easier to move an army. They also built strong walls as defensive barriers against barbarian attack, such as Hadrian's Wall in northern England. In many countries these barriers have survived the ravages and cataclysmic changes of the last 2,000 years.

I have in my library a copy of the classic Morgan Lectures of 1894, given at the Theological Seminary in Auburn, New York, by Dr. James Orr and entitled *The Neglected Factors of Church History.* Dr. Orr's purpose is to demonstrate the phenomenally rapid expansion of Christianity in Caesar's world. Let me share some of his findings.

First Dr. Orr traced the geographical expansion of Christianity. Everyone has heard of the catacombs under the city of Rome. They form a circle about three miles from the center of Rome. About forty chambers are known, connected to each other by a network of tunnels and secret passages. They were used as a Christian burial ground, and contain vast numbers of graves. According to Dr. Orr, forty separate Christian congregations were meeting in Rome just before the last persecution broke out. In Antioch, Syria, the church was estimated at 100,000 strong; in Asia Minor, it was estimated at one million, out of a total population of nineteen million.

Secondly, Orr investigated the influence of Christianity through the different levels of society. We know that the "common people heard him gladly" (Mark 12:37), but so did many of the wealthy, who attached themselves to the church, even in New Testament days. Jesus warned the rich against the dangers of relying on their wealth; James spoke of the man coming into the congregation wearing a gold ring; Luke spoke about those who were "possessors of lands or houses"; and Paul told Timothy to "charge them that are rich in this world" (Luke 6:24; James 2:2; Acts 4:34; 1 Timothy 6:17).

The church ministered to the needs of "widows," meaning women without financial support (Acts 6:1). Paul spoke about a salutation from "Caesar's household" (Philippians 4:22). Professor Harnack comments: "Between 50 and 60 years after Christianity reached Rome, a daughter of the Emperor (Vespasian) embraced the faith, and 30 years after the fearful persecutions of Nero, the presumptive heirs to the throne were brought up in a Christian house."

Finally, Dr. Orr traced Christianity's penetration of the thought patterns of society. As evidence, he refers to the books written by church leaders, and the special training in philosophy which was needed by the bishops of the early church. He also traces some of the converts' struggles for intellectual freedom in Christ. Justin Martyr, for example, dabbled in Platonic and other schools of philosophy, in his search for truth.

These, then, are some of the external factors leading to the rapid expansion of the Christian faith. But what of Christianity itself? What internal preparations did God make for the spread of His Word?

The apostles' achievement

After the ascension of Christ, the small Christian church in Jerusalem grew rapidly. But its success led to problems. After a few years, to avoid a possible breakaway by the Greek-speaking members of the church, seven deacons were appointed, all of whom had Greek names. Fragments survive of the story of only two: Philip and Stephen.

Philip preached and healed people in Samaria, and explained the Gospel to the Ethiopian eunuch (Acts 8:27–39).

Stephen preached with such power that he was taken prisoner and put on trial before the Sanhedrin, the Jewish council, where he accused the Jewish leaders of the murder of the Messiah. Quoting from comments made by Isaiah about the Temple, he argued that God dwells in no specific place on earth. The Pharisees, a fundamentalist group of

A view of St. Stephen's Gate to the Old City of Jerusalem, from the Mount of Olives. This is the traditional site of Stephen's martyrdom.

strict legalists, acknowledged Isaiah as inspired, and Stephen's interpretations enraged them. Dragging him outside the city walls, they stoned him to death, the first martyr of the Christian church.

A Pharisee, described as a "young man" in Acts 7:58, stood by and watched the killing, guarding the garments of the executioners. His name was Saul. For the rest of his life Saul was never able to escape the memory of the things he saw, heard and felt on that day. It was one of the goads which turned him towards Jesus, so that this most zealous of all persecutors of the church became the most impassioned of all followers of Christ. The church owes an everlasting debt of gratitude to that man, not only for his missionary activity but because, as "Paul," he wrote a large part of the New Testament. Who was he?

Paul's home was Tarsus in the Greek province of Cilicia. Tarsus was a university town, the home of philosophers, grammarians and poets. To have grown up in such a city must have contributed to his knowledge of the world and its thinking. His family, however, as he later told the Roman governor Agrippa, were the strictest Jews. Both Paul and his father were Pharisees, and he was fluent in the Hebrew language. He went to the Rabbinical College at Jerusalem for his training, and studied under the highly esteemed Gamaliel.

When Roman soldiers later put him in chains after a riot in the Temple in Jerusalem, Paul informed them that he was "a Roman," meaning that he held Roman citizenship. Their reaction to that information testifies to its value (Acts 22:25–29). This citizenship exempted Paul from slavery and excused him from degrading punishments such as scourging and crucifixion; it gave him the right to appeal to the Emperor against any lower court's decision; and, most important of all, it gave him the freedom to roam the world. He was, in every respect, the international man: Roman in his privileges, Jewish in his world view, and Greek in his thought patterns.

Paul became possessed of a passion to persecute Christians. After the death of Stephen, that thirst became insatiable. His hatred of Christians took him on a mission to Damascus, and on that journey he was dramatically converted to Christ. His passion never subsided; it was merely redirected.

Paul next spent some time—possibly as much as three years—in Arabia, pondering the issues involved in his conversion. Then he returned to Damascus and preached in the synagogue. His preaching infuriated the congregation, and they put a price on his head and a guard at every gate; but he escaped over the wall in a basket. With Barnabas, Paul spent a year in Antioch, a major provincial center, teaching the Christians there. It was the Christian church in Antioch which, under the direction of the Holy Spirit, sent off Paul and Barnabas to be pioneer missionaries.

Paul became a legend in his own day. He pioneered Gentile

The Library at Celsus, Ephesus. Paul spent two years in this prosperous city, encouraging the believers.

churches on two continents in the course of three if not four missionary journeys. He worked tirelessly for thirty years. His health was broken, his speech impeded, and it is probable that he had trouble with his eyes so that someone else had to write his letters for him. He traveled thousands of miles on both land and sea, in a day without the convenience of modern transportation. Probably most of his journeys were on foot. He was frequently at the center of riots, and at one of these his enemies stoned him and left him for dead. After twenty years, he reviewed his experiences in the following words:

In labours more abundant, in stripes above measure, in prisons more frequent, in deaths oft. Of the Jews five times received I forty stripes save one. Thrice was I beaten with rods, once was I stoned, thrice I suffered shipwreck, a night and a day I have been in the deep; in journeyings often, in perils of waters, in perils of robbers, in perils by mine own countrymen, in perils by the heathen, in perils in the city, in perils in the wilderness, in perils in the sea, in perils among false brethren; in weariness and painfulness, in watchings often, in hunger and thirst, in fastings often, in cold and nakedness. Beside those things that are without, that which cometh upon me daily, the care of all the churches (2 Corinthians 11:23–28).

And when he wrote this he had at least ten more years of ministry to endure. His traveling days ended when he was sent as a prisoner to Rome. But his missionary work continued. Though his body was manacled, his words could not be tied down.

The mighty pen

Part of the ancient Forum, Rome, center of a great Empire, and Paul's destination as a prisoner of Caesar.

Paul was a church planter and builder. On his first missionary journey, which took two and a half years, he covered 1,200 miles and visited different cities. He left new churches wherever he went. His ministry was so signally blessed that it provoked a debate among the church leaders in Jerusalem. He was required to appear before a Council presided over by James, the Lord's brother. During the debate, which focused on racial discrimination, truth was separated from prejudice, and the verdict exonerated Paul.

Paul's second missionary tour took three years and covered 2,800 miles—1,600 miles by land and another 1,200 miles by sea. It touched sixteen major cities in Asia and Europe, and resulted in the establishing of many new churches in Europe.

The third tour covered about 1,400 miles, and though it brought Paul to only three major cities and four provinces, in those provinces there were many cities through which he had previously passed, whose churches he must have visited again.

The Jews had been the divinely appointed writers and custodians of the Old Testament; now the church took over as custodians of the New Testament. Paul was the most prolific writer of all the New Testament authors, writing thirteen of the twenty-one New Testament letters. At least two of his letters were written during his second missionary journey, and three on his third. The rest were written either in prison, or between imprisonments. Towards the end of his life, Paul wrote the "Pastoral Letters" (1 and 2 Timothy, and Titus).

References in 2 Timothy and Titus suggest that Paul was exonerated at his first trial in Rome and then released, but later arrested and imprisoned again; so there were probably two imprisonments. It seems unlikely that he was in Rome in AD 64, when Nero set the city on fire and blamed the Christians, since, had he been in Rome at that time, he would most probably have suffered martyrdom with the other Christians. Perhaps he was in Spain, as he had already written that he intended to go on to Spain from Rome (Romans 15:24). Clement of Rome, Chrysostom and Jerome all refer to his visit to Spain, though without giving details. However, what we are sure about is that it was in Rome that Paul's earthly pilgrimage ended.

Paul's final prison in Rome may have been the Mamertine prison, a twenty-foot-deep hole in the ground into which the Romans dropped their prisoners through a hole in the ceiling—there were no stairs until medieval times. The Roman Senate met only fifty yards away from this spot. Beyond that was the Roman Forum, and Caesar's palace. The great imperial power transacted business above his cell.

When he arrived, he was "Paul the aged," crippled by chains and surrounded by soldiers. He was cold and asked for "the cloke that I left at Troas" (2 Timothy 4:13). He remarked that "Demas hath forsaken me"

(2 Timothy 4:10) and he urged Timothy not to be ashamed that Paul was a prisoner. He even informed Timothy, in his last letter, written from that cell, "at my first answer no man stood with me, but all men forsook me" (2 Timothy 4:16). Added to all this was his intuitive knowledge that his time on earth was finished: "I am now ready to be offered, and the time of my departure is at hand" (2 Timothy 4:6).

You can take a spiritual barometer reading on Paul as you read his last two letters, probably written from that dank, dark hole. Question him. Then listen to his replies.

"How are you doing, Paul?"

"Paul, an apostle of Jesus Christ [no fear in the presence of imperial Caesar], by the will of God [no revaluations because of adverse circumstances], according to the promise of life which is in Christ Jesus" (2 Timothy 1:1).

"Do you know that you are about to die?"

"I know whom I have believed, and am persuaded that he is able to keep that which I have committed unto him against that day . . . I have fought a good fight, I have finished my course, I have kept the faith" (2 Timothy 1:12, 4:7).

We leave Paul writing his last letters and move on. What happened to the New Testament writings after the first century?

Dangerous rip tides

Rip tides are generated by cross currents. In the second and third centuries spiritual rip tides occurred among Christians as conflicting outlooks met and clashed. Christianity emerged from a Jewish background, bringing with it a legalism which tried to direct its future course. At the same time, its converts were coming from a Greek background and, without adequate instruction, were introducing their mystical philosophies into the Christian assemblies. Both these currents of thought were at cross purposes with the true gospel. It was a dangerous time, a time of heresies and bitter conflict. These theological problems may seem dry to some people, but bear with me as I look at them because they were the means by which the infant church exercised its muscles and came to grips with what it believed. There were four categories of heresy:

Legalistic heresies
The main perpetrators of legalism were the Ebionites (the word means "poor men"), who survived for the first four centuries. Ebionites denied the deity of Christ, though they did accept Him as a prophet and Messiah. They taught that salvation was only possible through circumcision and obedience to the Law of Moses. This heresy forced the early church to focus clearly on the doctrine of salvation by grace, through faith.

Philosophical heresies

The first and greatest of the philosophical threats to the early church was known as Gnosticism. According to Irenaeus (who lived from about AD 130 to about AD 200), this heresy began with Simon Magus, whom Peter rebuked (Acts 8), and reached its peak about AD 150. The word "Gnostic" comes from a Greek word meaning "knowledge." Gnostics believed that salvation was achieved through secret knowledge of one's true nature, only available to an inner group of believers.

A fundamental tenet of Gnosticism was the view that "spirit" was holy while "matter" was evil. A corollary of this was the teaching that Christ could not have had a physical body. Supporters of this heresy were called "Docetists" (from the Greek word *doces*, "to seem"). Docetists argued either that Christ's body was a phantom—it appeared to be a human body but was not—or else that He used a human carcass between His baptism and His crucifixion, but was separate from it. In either case, Christ Himself did not experience physical suffering.

There was a Syrian form of the heresy, differing from an Egyptian form and another form in Asia Minor, under the leadership of Marcion. Marcion interests us because he rejected the Old Testament and collected the earliest known Christian canon, which included a shortened form of Luke's Gospel and ten of Paul's letters. This directed attention to the question of which books belong to the canon of scripture.

Theological heresies

The main theological heresies were Montanism (which appeared about AD 170) and Monarchianism (a third-century heresy). Montanus was a charismatic prophet who opposed the formalism creeping into the church. He taught that the Spirit speaks to his church today, just as he did through Paul and the other apostles, and, moreover, has new revelations to give. Followers of Montanus accepted his extravagant teaching that Jesus was coming back to his region to give him a prominent place in His future kingdom. They also practiced a strict asceticism.

Monarchianism was an ancient form of Unitarianism. It stemmed from an over-zealous defense of the unity of God. Monarchians maintained that He was not three persons but one God. Consequently they taught that Christ was not divine, but merely a good man. It was over this subject that the church fought its first major battle, known as the Arian Controversy.

A strong proponent of Monarchianism was Paul of Samosata, Bishop of Antioch from 260 to 272, who held an important political post in the government of Zenobia, Queen of Palmyra. He preached with violent gestures, asking for applause and getting the people to wave their handkerchiefs. He was condemned as a heretic by a synod of Antioch in 268.

Opposite: Ruins of the ancient theater at Hierapolis, Asia Minor. Papias, first Bishop of Hierapolis, knew the apostle John.

Ecclesiastical schisms

It is one of the strange phenomena of church history that members of a newly fledged group, attacked by brutal and powerful forces and facing the threat of extinction, could yet find something to disagree about among themselves. For example, Christians fought over when Easter should be celebrated. Christ rose on Sunday, the 14th of Nisan. When 14th Nisan was not a Sunday, should 14th Nisan be celebrated as Easter Day, or the nearest Sunday? The disagreement was not settled until the Council of Nicaea in 325.

A more serious disagreement caused the Donatist schism—which happened in North Africa after the persecutions had passed. The problem was that in 312 Caecilian had been ordained Bishop of Carthage by Felix, a bishop who had handed over his Bible to be burned during the Diocletian persecution ten years earlier. Could Caecilian be accepted as a bishop when he had been ordained by someone who had failed under pressure? Many North African Christians felt no ordination had taken place, and elected Donatus to be bishop in Caecilian's place. Donatists—followers of Donatus—regarded themselves as the true church, and the Christian church had to decide on what grounds they were mistaken.

Paradoxically, all these conflicts within the Christian church served a beneficial purpose. Just as germs give rise to antibodies, which make the human body healthier, so heresies left the Christian church stronger. False theologies gave birth to Christian theology, and conflict forced the development of an authoritative creed, as well as the desire for a canon of scripture.

Standing in the gap

While Jesus lived, He was the sole voice of authority. After His departure, apostles became the authority, and their ministry was confirmed with outward signs given by the Spirit of God. The search for a replacement for Judas revealed the qualifications of an apostle: apostles were eyewitnesses. They were men who had been with Jesus throughout His ministry and had witnessed the resurrection (Acts 1:22). This was the apostolic period.

When the apostles died, we enter the post-apostolic period. Now the men who counted were those who had *known* the apostles. In the post-apostolic era, there were threats to the unity of the church, the purity of its doctrine and the authority of the Bible. Three men in particular withstood these attacks. The first was Papias, Bishop of Hierapolis in Phrygia, about AD 130. He knew the apostle John, and Philip's four daughters. Though his writings have been lost, they were quoted by his contemporaries, and from them we learn useful information about the apostles and the origins of the Gospels. For example, we learn that Mark was Peter's traveling companion and interpreter, and "wrote down

Polycarp, the eighty-six-year-old martyr who refused to renounce his Savior.

accurately all that Peter recorded of the words and deeds of the Lord, though not in strict order.''

The second witness was Polycarp, a contemporary of Papias. Polycarp was a disciple of the apostle John and was appointed pastor of the church at Smyrna. He wrote a letter to the church at Philippi that is saturated with the language of the New Testament books. He quoted from most of the New Testament letters and also from the four Gospels—which shows that they were written and recognised as authoritative in the mid-second century. Polycarp was put to death at the stake for refusing to curse Christ. His words are unforgettable: ''I have served Him for eighty-six years, and He never did me any wrong: how can I blaspheme my King and my Savior?''

The third of these witnesses was Clement of Rome, bishop of the church in Rome at the end of the first century. He knew many of the apostles, and may have been the Clement referred to by Paul in Philippians 4:3. From Clement's letter to the Corinthian church, written about AD 96, we may infer that the Christians in Rome were beginning to gather together the scattered New Testament books. Clement had access to some Gospel writings, Paul's letter to the Romans, and 1 Corinthians, as well as one or two of Paul's other letters, 1 Peter, and the letter to the Hebrews.

Defending the faith

When these men died, around AD 150, another group had to struggle with the problems of leadership and authority. They cover the next 150 years and fall into two categories: Apologists and Polemicists. Apologists were concerned with non-Christians in the Roman Empire, while Polemicists were concerned with the church; Apologists defended Christian conduct, Polemicists defended Christian doctrine. They were two sides of the same coin.

Top: Justin Martyr (c100–c165); *bottom:* Tertullian (c150–222).

Apologists had two tasks. Negatively, they refuted false accusations such as cannibalism, incest and antisocial action. Positively, they compared Christianity favourably with Judaism, paganism and the state religion of the empire. Two examples suffice to introduce them.

Justin Martyr was probably the foremost apologist of the second century. He was born in Neapolis in Samaria about AD 100, and became a wandering philosopher, dabbling in Stoic philosophy and the idealism of Plato. One day, while he was walking by the sea shore, an old man advised him to examine the writings of the apostles; these led him to Christ. Justin Martyr wrote two major works, the first of which he addressed to the Emperor Marcus Aurelius. About AD 165 he was beheaded in Rome for his faith.

The second major apologist was Tertullian, born about AD 150 in Carthage. Learned in the classical languages, he was converted to Christ while practicing as a lawyer in Rome. In his *Apologeticus*, addressed to the Roman governor of his province, he upheld the innocence of Christians of the crimes attributed to them, and pointed out that persecution was a failure since Christians increased rapidly in number during every surge of hostility. Tertullian is credited with saying that "the blood of the martyrs is the seed of the church," and is considered the father of Latin theology.

Polemicists defended Christianity against the speculative theologies of mysticism. They fought the beliefs from which they themselves had been converted, and by maintaining orthodoxy they saved the church from calamity. These men include Irenaeus (c130–c200), who opposed the Gnostic heresy, and Clement of Alexandria (c150–c215) (not to be

Origen (c185–254), scholar and Christian apologist.

confused with Clement of Rome), who became the head of a training school in Alexandria, until forced by persecution to retire. Clement was widely read in Greek pagan literature and is said to have quoted from as many as 500 different sources.

We dare not miss Origen (c185–254), who was one of the greatest thinkers and scholars of his day, both as an apologist and as a polemicist. His father was martyred in Alexandria, when he was sixteen, leaving him to support a family of six. Origen was determined to die with his father, and his mother had to hide his clothes to prevent him leaving the house. He was not only a theologian but also a man of deep spirituality and faith.

What was the contribution of these men to the indestructible Book? The story is told of a group of British scholars at a dinner party, back in the eighteenth century, who entertained themselves by posing questions. The question came up, "What if the New Testament had been successfully destroyed, as was attempted by the emperors? Could we have recovered it through the writings of the apologists and polemicists?" Two months later, Sir David Dalrymple, who had been present, called a meeting at his home. On a table sat a heap of musty volumes, to which he pointed, saying, "These are some of those writings of the second and third centuries. I have examined them and, so far, I have recovered the entire New Testament, with the exception of eleven verses."

The blood of the martyrs . . . the seed of the church

The infamous Colosseum was begun by Vespasian in AD 72 and completed by his son Titus in AD 80. It stood until the Normans sacked Rome in 1084, and now all that remains is its skeleton. In it a noble army of Christian martyrs gave up their life to satisfy the blood-lust of the Roman mob. When Rome was on holiday, great crowds would converge on the arena, hungry for thrills, and when the holidays were over, the janitors would calmly lock the sated lions back in their cellars, and clear the carnage of human flesh. The Colosseum symbolizes conflict and sacrifice, one of the dark pages of history, when early Christianity witnessed the fury of pagan hostility.

But why was this? Why were Christians on the receiving end of such animosity? There were a number of reasons. The first was political. The one unifying factor in the vast Roman Empire, with its multiplicity of nationalities and religions, was worship of the Emperor. With the exception of the Jews, everyone had to offer incense to the genius of the Emperors. Not to do so was treason. For a long time Christians were thought to be members of a Jewish sect. Eventually the Roman authorities realized that Jews hated Christians. When Christians nevertheless refused to honor the Emperor, and met in clandestine places at night, they came under suspicion of hatching a conspiracy.

The second reason was religious. The Romans believed in a plurality of gods, so they were happy to put another idol among the rest at the Pantheon, as long as it was subordinate to the Roman state religion. But the Christian God would not fit on an idol shelf. Moreover, the Romans resented the exclusiveness of Christianity, and suspected it to be a cloak for evil religious rites.

The Colosseum, Rome, where many a Christian was martyred to assuage the crowd's bloodlust.

Christianity was also out of place socially. It taught a concept of human equality that put emperors and slaves on the same level, beneath a higher power. It is easy to see how this could unnerve the rulers of an Empire of which half the population were slaves.

Finally, there were economic reasons for hostility to the church. We see this in Acts 19. The craftsmen in Ephesus who made the little black idols of Diana lost their income when sales dropped. They did not engineer a riot out of moral or spiritual outrage, but because their pockets suffered. Multiply that throughout the Empire and you can see the magnitude of the threat to Christians.

At first active persecution was confined to the local level, the result of local conditions and the character of the governor, but after 250 it became empire-wide. Sometimes persecution was led by a particular emperor, and relief came at that emperor's death. The first time the imperial power turned on Christians was after the great fire of Rome in

**The Roman Emperor Nero
(AD 37–68), whose cruelty has
become the stuff of legend.**

AD 64. The Roman historian Tacitus reported: "Rome being set on fire, Nero declared it was the work of the Christians and put great numbers of them to death, after frightful tortures." Other historians tell of the "troublesome coat" the Christians were made to wear. It was made of coarse cloth, besmeared with pitch, wax and sulphur. Dressed in this coat, they were hung by their chins from sharp stakes fixed in the ground, and set on fire. Nero had them burned at midnight "for torches to the city."

Why were Christians executed with such cruelty and bitterness during these persecutions? Stories are told of houses that were filled with Christians, and then burned to the ground. Groups of fifty people were tied with ropes, and then forced into the sea. Swords, red-hot chairs, wheels for stretching human bodies, and talons of iron to tear them were all used by pagan Rome in the effort to stamp out the influence of One who was "meek and lowly of heart."

The final wave of persecution came in March 303, in an edict issued by the Emperor Diocletian, calling for an end to all Christian meetings and the destruction of church buildings and of all sacred writings. Eusebius, the church historian, wrote that a later edict, issued in 304, ordered Christians to sacrifice to the pagan gods or be put to death. He also reported that the prisons became so crowded that there was no room to accommodate the criminals. In many places officials turned a blind eye to Christians who did not throw incense on the altar. But persecution was particularly bad in Egypt and Palestine, where it increased in ferocity after Diocletian's abdication in 305. Eventually Galerius issued an edict from his deathbed in 311, giving toleration to Christianity; in 313 the Edict of Milan was issued, bringing freedom of worship to Christianity, as well as to all other religions.

A survey of the years between 64 and 305 brings three conclusions. First, as we have seen, "the blood of the martyrs was the seed of the church." Christianity did not merely survive the persecutions, it thrived. In the middle of the first century Christianity was strong in Palestine, and its center was Jerusalem. By the end of the first century it had taken root across the Roman Empire. By the end of the third century it had penetrated the remotest corners of the Empire—and beyond—and in some parts of the Roman Empire Christians were even in a majority.

Secondly, the persecution sharpened people's perceptions of the church. Those who compromised caused anguished debate: were they fit to worship with those who stood loyal to the cause? As they faced the prospects of torture and martyrdom, Christians were provoked to question the priorities of life: is life more sacred than truth? Are family ties secondary to the ties of the family of God?

Thirdly, persecution focused attention on the authority of the Word of God. It had not yet been finally agreed which books were to be accepted as divinely inspired. But the process had begun.

2. The Bible in the Middle Ages

(about AD 500–1500)

Pandora's box

Constantine, the son of a co-emperor, was brought up at the emperor's court. He joined his father, who was responsible for Spain, Gaul and Britain, in a war against the Picts and they were in York when in 306 his father died. Constantine was acclaimed as emperor by the army, but Rome would only recognize him as Caesar (deputy emperor). At the battle of Milvian Bridge, by the walls of Rome, in 312, Constantine defeated the western emperor, Maxentius, and became Caesar Augustus

Constantine the Great, whose edict of toleration marked the end of official persecution of the church.

of the western Empire. On the eve of this battle, on a bright afternoon, he claimed he saw the sign of the cross in the sky, bearing the inscription "By this sign conquer." He claimed that the following night the Lord came to him in a dream and commanded him to mark his soldier's shields with the first two Greek letters of the name of Christ, and to use these letters, combined with the cross, as his standard. Thus was Constantine's supposed conversion, reported to us by the Christian historian, Eusebius, many years later.

In January 313, Constantine published a memorable "edict of toleration", by which all religious cults were to be tolerated. It also required the return of all Christian property that had been confiscated and gave Christians access to public office. This edict did not make Christianity the religion of the Empire—but it did mark the beginning of the downfall of paganism.

Constantine was not baptized until he fell sick in 337, the same year that he died. The Senate of Rome placed him among the gods, and to this day the Greek and Russian Orthodox Churches celebrate his festival on May 21.

Constantine married the church to the state; but it was the state that was the head, and the church subordinate. This harmful alliance persisted for more than 1,000 years.

Constantine's personal life was not consistent with his profession of faith. He was overwhelmingly conceited, and gathered around him those who fed his ego. He was egocentric enough to think that God had revealed Himself to him in a unique way, as though God had made special efforts to convert him. Even the bishops of his court often forgot which ruler was their master. One of them told Constantine he was appointed by God to be the ruler over all, and designated to reign with the Son of God in the world to come. To his credit, Constantine reminded the bishop to restrain his language and pray for him.

Constantine was also prey to fits of jealousy and anger. He had his second wife, Fausta, and his step-son, Crispus, put to death because he was suspicious of them. His decision, however, was based on misinformation, and he regretted it later.

His priorities were misconceived. He considered affluence the sign of divine approval. He took bishops who had been reduced to relative poverty, scarred and dazed from the recent persecutions, and brought them into palaces that blazed with light and breathed with perfume. His attitude toward the power of wealth is seen in his actions after the destruction of the pagan temple at Heliopolis, with its abominable and licentious rites. Though there were no Christians in the region, he built a church in place of the pagan temple and staffed it with clergymen and a bishop. Then he bestowed large sums of wealth on it for the support of the poor, assuming that this would produce conversions. Here we see the beginnings of the shift from Christ to cash, from preaching to purchasing, which was later to dominate much of the medieval church.

Constantine's theology was also lacking. He struggled to free himself from a dreadful horror of demons. When his conscience bothered him over the murder of his step-son, he turned for help first to a Platonic philosopher, and then to some heathen priests. It was some time later that he was informed that the Christian faith had a solution for *every* sin.

One benefit did come from Constantine's association with the Christian church. In 331, the emperor asked Eusebius to prepare fifty copies of the Bible for use in the churches of Constantinople, with the result that attention was again directed to the issue of what constitutes the Bible.

The Creed

There are two periods in church history in which general Councils attempted to define dogma. The first period stretched from 325 to 787, when seven ecumenical Councils were held; the second was during the time of the Reformation in the sixteenth century.

In 324 Constantine had defeated Licinius, the head of the eastern Empire, and now ruled a united Empire from Constantinople. He was determined to have his subjects united in the worship of God, but he faced a difficult task. The Christian church was seething with bitter theological disputes. Deep splits and fractures made unity a seemingly impossible dream. The Councils were called in an attempt to resolve these disagreements. The first and last were held in the city of Nicaea, and all seven dealt with differences about the doctrine of the Trinity. Here is the story behind the first ecumenical Council.

Alexander, the bishop of Alexandria in 318, preached a sermon on the unity of the Trinity in which he said that "Christ" was the name given to the Father in His role on earth. A presbyter named Arius, who was a popular local preacher, heard the sermon and strongly disagreed on the grounds that the bishop failed to distinguish between Christ and the Father. Arius believed that Christ was less than divine, though more than man. The conflict became so sharp that Alexander had Arius condemned by a church council, and excommunicated.

Alexander refused to allow any follower of Arius to come to the Lord's table. He was adamant. He simply would not break bread with anyone who denied the deity of Christ. The dispute developed into a question of salvation: could anyone less than God deliver sinners from their just doom?

Arius fled to the East, and found refuge with a preacher by the name of Eusebius—not the historian, who was the Bishop of Caesarea, but an old school friend. Here in the East his views were more acceptable: the church at Antioch, in its attempt to resist the heresy of making Christ a mere emanation of the Father, had long stressed his humanity. The

Top: Arius, whose controversial view of the Trinity was debated at the Council of Nicaea in AD 325.
Bottom: Eusebius, Bishop of Nicaea, and first great historian of the church.

Athanasius (293–373), Arius' chief opponent at Nicaea.

dispute continued, creating a theological cleavage between the Eastern and Western churches. Believing that it might cause a serious schism, the emperor attempted to mediate.

Constantine wrote a letter to both parties, chastening them for disputing rash, speculative questions which he considered did not affect the essence of Christianity. But the debate was too profound to be resolved in such a simple manner. The emperor therefore called for a general Council of all representatives of the Christian church. This first ever ecumenical Council met at Nicaea in north-west Asia Minor in AD 325.

Nearly three hundred bishops came, some from Eastern churches beyond the Roman Empire, but only a handful from the West. The bishop of Rome sent two presbyters in his place. The emperor presided over the gathering, paying all the expenses. There were three prominent voices, expressing three different viewpoints. First there was Arius. He contended that Christ was not eternal, but was created by God before time. Christ was not "coequal, coeternal and consubstantial" with the Father. Second, there was a young man, just over thirty, from a wealthy background, trained at the school of Alexandria. His name was Athanasius. He was present merely as a deacon, aiding his bishop. He ably defended what we consider to be the orthodox view, that Christ was eternal, and of the same substance as the Father.

The third voice was that of the historian Eusebius, the Bishop of Caesarea, and his was the majority party. He attempted a compromise position, trying to link what he considered to be the good points of both Arius and Athanasius. Eusebius brought with him a copy of the baptismal confession of his own church at Caesarea to which the bishops of his area subscribed. It was perfectly orthodox—but did not answer the questions under dispute. Since it left a certain vagueness, allowing the different parties to interpret according to their own views, it was acceptable to the Alexandrian school, provided that a condemnation of Arianism be appended. After a brief dispute, this was agreed, four anathemas against all who supported an Arian position were added to Eusebius' creed. Eusebius at first fought the additions, but later he yielded for the sake of peace. But the truce was temporary.

The enemy, having failed to destroy the church through persecution, was now adopting different tactics: he was attempting to dismantle Christianity through internal schisms.

Nicaea's solution to church problems failed. Constantine came to support Arius, whom he believed to be orthodox. He could not understand Athanasius' refusal to countenance Arianism. The controversy caused great bitterness for the next fifty-one years, until, at the next major ecumenical Council in Constantinople in 381, it was decided that what the bishops had voted in 325 "shall not be set aside." That decision was later approved at the Council of Chalcedon in 451. So the Creed of

Nicaea became the legal, orthodox religion.

Nicaea strengthened the state-church relationship. The emperor called the meeting, paid its expenses, presided over its deliberations and, according to Eusebius, decided its outcome. Eventually a bishop would take over the authority of the Emperor, exercising catholic authority in all matters civic and sacred.

But good came out of the Council's deliberations. It emphasized that Bible and creed complement each other. In Ephesians 6, Paul writes of the "girdle of truth" and "the sword of the Spirit." The former is the creed, and the latter is the Word. The first without the second is impossible, and the second without the first is dangerous. One of the difficulties that faced these early church theologians was that they were dealing with issues not clearly defined in the Scriptures—for example, the relationships of Father, Son and Holy Spirit in the Godhead, and the deity and humanity of Christ. But one thing was clear: what they were fighting over was the meaning of Scripture. The writings of the apostles formed the highest court of appeal on all matters of faith and practice.

The New Testament canon

When we refer to a "canon" we are simply talking about a measuring rod, a plumb line, or acceptable weights used to balance scales. The word was first applied to the scriptures in the fourth century. But the New Testament canon did not come together in one single event. It was a slow process which began about thirty years after Jesus died and continued for four hundred years.

What made a book "canonical"? There were a number of factors. First, that the book was written by an apostle, or authorized by an apostle; second, that its teaching honored Christ, and was consistent with the teaching of the apostles; third, that it had been acknowledged and used by Christians since the earliest days of the church.

The formation of the canon went through a number of stages.

1. The early church believed the time was short, and Jesus was coming "quickly." They did not want to waste time writing instead of preaching.

2. As time passed, people wrote down the gist of the message (which was all that was required to lead someone to Christ). Accuracy of words, with their tenses and syntax, was at this stage unnecessary.

3. Then came the Diocletian persecution in 303, which called for the burning of all sacred writings. We do not know how many copies were destroyed during this time; it must have been thousands. This made people more aware of the importance of the New Testament writings.

4. Replacing the destroyed copies, as well as catering for the numerical and geographical expansion of the church, brought a flood of documents into circulation. Constantine, for example, as we have seen, asked

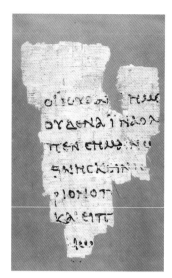

The John Rylands Fragment, the oldest known manuscript of the Gospels.

for fifty copies of the Bible to take to the churches at Constantinople. It has been estimated that there are 13,000 extant documents which purport to be copies of the sacred writings; of these, 8,000 were written in Latin, and 5,000 in Greek.

5. Controversial theologies could only be tested against authoritative writings. The period of apostolic authority had passed, the age of papal authority had not yet been born; only the Writings had the authority to settle a dispute.

Reaching agreement

The first five books of the New Testament, Matthew through Acts, were generally accepted from the outset. Inasmuch as Christianity is Christ, what else could have been deemed necessary other than the unveiling of Him? By the end of the first century, the four Gospels had been collected together, as had Paul's letters. The introduction of codices (meaning books in our modern form, as opposed to scrolls) early in the second century allowed such collections to be included in one volume—it had not been possible to write so much material on to one scroll. But there was no general acceptance of 2 and 3 John, 2 Peter, Jude and Revelation until the fourth century. Even then, Hebrews was still not included because of doubts about its authorship. With the growing separation between East and West, there was disagreement on whether any other books should be included: some wanting the *Epistle of Clement*, and also another Epistle named after Barnabas, and the *Shepherd* of Hermas.

The first attempt at a list of New Testament writings comes from the heretic Marcion, about AD 140. As we have seen, this stimulated the church to provide its own, orthodox, canon. We learn from the writings of Tertullian that about AD 150 a collection of New Testament writings, virtually the same as our New Testament, was accepted as authoritative at Rome.

The first orthodox list that we possess also stems from Rome. It dates between AD 170 and 210, and is known as the "Muratorian Fragment." The copy we have was written in Latin and, because of its antiquity, it is an important document. It omits the books of Hebrews and James, the letters of Peter, and one of John's letters. It also rejects two manuscripts which were circulating in the period—a letter to the Laodiceans, and another one to the Alexandrians but it accepts the apocryphal *Wisdom of Solomon* and *Apocalypse of Peter*.

Origen, writing about AD 230, gives us a list of books that without dispute belonged to Scripture. His list agrees with the Muratorian Fragment, and adds Hebrews, 2 Peter, 2 and 3 John, James and Jude.

In the fourth century our present list of twenty-seven books is cited by Athanasius in the East (AD 367) and by Jerome and Augustine in the West. Athanasius was considered the greatest theologian of his day.

A page from the Codex Sinaiticus, one of the most important documents for establishing an accurate text for our Bible today.

Shortly after his twentieth birthday, he plunged into writing, leaving a memorable theological treatise on the doctrine of redemption. When Alexander, the Bishop of Alexandria, died in 328, Athanasius succeeded him.

Carthage, in North Africa, was a famous city which was a significant political rival to Rome. By the fourth century, though Carthage was politically less important, the Christian church there continued to take the lead among the African churches. Between 218 and 418, fourteen Councils were held at Carthage, the majority debating issues related to baptism. But the eighth Council of Carthage, which met in 397, confirmed the canon of twenty-seven New Testament books, ratifying a decision made four years earlier at the North African synod of Hippo and endorsing the accepted practice of the Catholic church.

The church now possessed a voice of authority equivalent to that of Jesus while He was living on earth. To this authority every council or conclave, every priest or pope, every deliberative body or denominational body must bow. This Word is supreme!

Idolizing the Book

Eusebius Hieronymus, better known to us simply as Jerome, was born in Dalmatia in 331, to Christian parents. His early education was supervised by his father, who later sent him to Rome to study rhetoric and philosophy under the great teacher Donatus. While he was in Rome he submitted to baptism, and to a serious commitment to a life of rigid abstinence.

In 373, Jerome set out with three friends for Palestine, stopping at Antioch on his way. While he was there he caught a severe fever. During his illness he had a dream in which Christ said to him: "You are not a Christian." It so sobered him that he gave up the study of worldly books and went into the desert for about four years. Here he improved his knowledge of Greek and set about learning Hebrew, a language known by few, if any, Western theologians. After this he returned to Antioch where he was ordained priest in 378. In 379 he traveled to Constantinople to study under Gregory Nazianzen and became close friends with him. Influenced by Gregory's sermons against Arianism, Jerome became a conscientious contender for truth against error. He translated some of the Greek writings of Eusebius and Origen. Two years later, he returned to Rome, where Damasus was bishop. From the moment the two men met, a warm and lasting friendship developed between them, and Jerome became secretary to Damasus. Jerome hated the soft, indulgent lifestyle and lax morals of many of the Christians in Rome, and was openly critical of the Roman church—so much so that after the death of Damasus he was asked to leave.

Jerome, whose translation of the Old and New Testaments became known as the Vulgate.

There was a most significant outcome of Jerome's three-year stay in Rome. Until the middle of the third century the western churches spoke Greek. Only in North Africa was Latin regularly used. By the fourth century, however, Latin was the language of communication for both church and Empire. By the time of Jerome there were many Latin translations of different parts of the New Testament, but few were reliable. So Damasus asked Jerome to revise the Latin New Testament. His Gospels appeared in 384, and were followed shortly by the rest of the New Testament. His revision, though excellent, was much criticised—people hated to see their favorite verses changed—and this was a further reason why he was asked to leave Rome.

From Rome he moved to Bethlehem, to live a monastic life and dedicate himself to the enormous undertaking of revising the Latin Old Testament. He faced a hopeless task. In North Africa the existing Latin translation was based, not on the original Hebrew, but on the Greek Septuagint, and it had many weaknesses. For example, it was the work of many different people, with the result that the same Hebrew words were translated inconsistently. After a while Jerome abandoned his revision of this Latin translation and turned directly to the Hebrew. Another Bible had appeared among Eastern churches: Origen's Hexapla. This

Pope Damasus (c304–384), who, with Jerome's help, promulgated the canon of Scripture, and commissioned Jerome to translate the Vulgate.

comprised the Old Testament, written in six columns: the first column in Hebrew, and the other five in variant Greek translations. Jerome's assignment was to take Origen's Hebrew text and translate it directly into Latin.

In the year 405 his mission was complete, but he spent the rest of his life in Bethlehem, dedicating himself to writing defenses of the orthodox faith. During his controversy with the Pelagians, his life was threatened, and he had to flee from Bethlehem. He left for two years, returning in 418, two years before he died.

Some people had assumed that Jerome was correcting the Septuagint, thereby criticising the seventy-two scholars who had made this

Antony of Egypt, an early hermit in the desert, who acted as spiritual director to other monks.

translation, and they opposed what they regarded as Jerome's insolent revision. But Jerome's translation both of the Old and New Testaments was far superior to all existing Latin translations. Scholars such as Augustine accepted it and soon it was introduced into all the churches of the West. The majority of scholars considered his work "an immortal service" which placed him "above all his contemporaries, and even all his successors down to the sixteenth century. Jerome, by his linguistic knowledge, his oriental travel, and his entire culture, was best fitted, and in fact the only man to undertake and successfully execute so gigantic a task."

His work became known as the "Vulgate," or Bible "in the common language," but paradoxically it turned out to be the very instrument which blocked the road to any other vulgate. It was so highly esteemed that succeeding generations decided to forbid anyone to make any other translation, and Latin became the official language of religion, with priests, whatever their mother tongue, being taught in Latin. So the good became the enemy of the best, and ordinary people, who did not know Latin, were deprived of a Bible. The fall of the Roman Empire in the fifth century sent Europe plunging into the darkness of the Middle Ages, a darkness that was made all the deeper by the absence of a Bible and biblical teaching for the masses.

The movement in the monastery

Though there were ascetic communities in Judea before the time of Christ, Jesus was not an ascetic, and as far as we know there were no monks in the very early years of Christianity. The first monks lived alone (the word comes from a Greek word meaning "people who live alone") and monasticism as we know it did not begin to take shape until the middle of the third century. The change began with Antony who for twenty years lived a solitary life in the desert in Upper Egypt. Gradually other Christians followed his example and came to live in the same area. Though they lived as hermits, Antony acted as their spiritual director.

The first monastic community was established by Pachomius at Tabennisi on the Nile, where a group of hermits lived together with a common "rule." The practice was encouraged and developed by Basil (329–389) in Cappadocia in western Asia.

A monastery became a self-contained society, under the umbrella of the church, dedicated to the maintenance of a specific doctrine or practice. The words of Jesus on the distribution of wealth, and inferences made from Paul's teaching on celibacy in marriage were common arguments for the defense of monasticism.

Monasticism in Palestine began about 315, introduced there by Hilarion, who had been influenced by Antony in Egypt. Athanasius, who was a friend and supporter of Antony, introduced the idea to

Christians in Rome during a visit in 340. As we have seen, when Jerome came to Rome in 382 he became deeply disturbed by the influence of secular life on the church. Excessive opulence, on the one hand, and authoritarian leadership, on the other, were leading to a drift away from piety and moral integrity. Jerome became a preacher of monasticism, and an advocate of sanctity and abstinence. He was opposed by the clergy, though he enlisted some notable converts, most of whom were widows and daughters of the wealthy. An outstanding convert, Paula, was heir to a fortune which she distributed among the poor. Her son-in-law was a senator who was also converted to Jerome's teaching. When Jerome moved to Bethlehem, the women followed him, and Paula founded four convents in Palestine, three for nuns and one for monks, which she placed under the care of Jerome. According to the church historian Philip Schaff, Jerome was the father of Roman monasticism. The practice soon flourished from Asia Minor to Britain.

At the beginning of the sixth century, Benedict founded a monastic order which became the pattern for western monasticism. His Benedictine monastery was to be "a school of the service of the Lord." Because the system involved no rigid central control but rather a loose federation of autonomous abbeys under "abbots," there were several offshoots, each differing on some matter and forming a new order. Monastic orders sprang up like denominations in Protestantism, each one having some point of difference in theology or practice.

By 1100, monasticism was on the defensive. Land and other forms of wealth had been donated to the monasteries, and it was no longer only the pious who were attracted to monastic life: secular greed in sacred garb started grabbing the wealth.

Towards the end of the Middle Ages another reform occurred. This was the birth of the friars (the word means "brother")—the Carmelites (founded in 1154), Franciscans and Dominicans (founded early in the thirteenth century), and several varieties of Augustinians. While the monk operated within the confines of the monastery; the friar brought religion out to the community. The friars held no property, but worked or begged for their living. Within one generation, the two great founders, Dominic (c1170–1221) and Francis (c1182–1226), had died; but their influence spread rapidly and far, bringing a new transfusion of life into the monastic orders.

The abbeys became the salt of the secular world. Benedict had worked out detailed job descriptions for all members of the monastic community. The monks were engaged in prayer and praise both day and night but they had secular, as well as sacred, work. Their secular employment gave them independence from feudal lords and maintained their commitment to the monastery.

The monasteries were also educational centers, the monks and friars being employed in writing, and copying classical works of philosophy and literature. Only with the rise of cathedral schools and universities at the end of the Middle Ages did their educational supremacy die down.

But the most important service performed by monasteries lay in the study and copying of scripture. They kept the Word of God alive, and monasteries were bright centers in a dark world.

But important as monasteries were, like the priest, the monk stood between the peasant and his God. As we have seen, the Bible was out of the reach of ordinary men and women, whose approach to truth was mediated through priest and monk.

Life on the fringe

St. Patrick, the celebrated monk from Ireland.

The introduction of Christianity to the fringes of the empire is most interesting, and many stories and legends have come down to us. In one such story, we are told of a philosopher from Tyre, named Meropius, who set out to sail to India. Shipwrecked off the coast of Abyssinia, he and all his party were executed by the natives. The sole survivors were two boys, who were spared because of their tender age. They were sent as slaves to the king, and served him well enough to become his cupbearers. On the king's death, they were granted their freedom and the widowed queen asked them to take charge of her son. They gained such influence that they were able to establish Christianity in the country and one of them later traveled to Alexandria to ask Athanasius to send bishops back to Abyssinia. In this way Christianity gained a foothold in that distant country. However, our interest lies in the rise of the English Bible.

Ireland

Though much of our knowledge of St. Patrick is conjectural, we know he was born in 389 somewhere along the west coast of Britain. His father was reputed to have been a wealthy church deacon, and Patrick was educated and disciplined as a Christian, but he tells us that he himself was not a Christian. When he was sixteen, a band of Irish marauders plundered his neighbourhood and, along with his father's men and maid servants and thousands of other people, Patrick was taken captive to Ireland, a country which was never part of the Roman Empire. They were sold as slaves, and Patrick spent the next six years serving as the chieftain's shepherd. He wrote later that it was during this time that "The Lord opened the understanding of my unbelief . . . that I might turn to the Lord my God." His faith kept him alive, and eventually, following God's inner voice, he escaped. He found his way to the sea and sailed from Ireland with a group of sea traders who were exporting Irish wolf-dogs. Three days later they landed in France and traveled for another two months before Patrick left them for the monastery of Lérins, where he became a monk. After several years, he left the Mediterranean area and returned to Britain. In a dream, he saw a man named Victorinus carrying some parchments, one of which he held up to Patrick. The parchment began, "The voice of Ireland." He heard someone call, "Patrick, holy boy, come and walk among us again."

Against the strongest urging of friends, he determined to go to Ireland and spent the next fourteen years at Auxerre in preparation for his missionary vocation. He was ordained as a deacon, and eventually consecrated bishop and allowed to set sail. His exploits were numerous, and the subject of many myths. His major work seems to have been in the north where, as the Bishop of Armagh, he retired in 461. The gospel had already reached Ireland before Patrick's missionary work there, but it was because of Patrick that the Christian message spread throughout the whole country. Because of him Ireland became a land of "saints and scholars," and missionaries went out from Ireland to the Anglo-Saxon kingdoms.

Scotland

In 521, Columba was born in Ireland. By 544, he received his priest's orders, and he is believed to have founded the monasteries of Derry. In 563, when he was forty-two years old, he set sail with twelve companions in a frail boat made of wicker covered with hides. They landed on the Isle of Iona, off the Island of Mull, in western Scotland. The island is only three miles long and a mile and a half wide, and even today has fewer than 300 inhabitants. Columba built a monastery on the island, and from there he preached the gospel to the Picts. He is reputed to have died on June 9, 597. So the gospel came to Scotland and, like Ireland, without any help from the church at Rome.

The ancient Celtic church on Iona, where Columba built his monastery in the sixth century.

52

An artist's impression of the Irish missionary Columba (521–597).

Britain

Caesar had conquered Britain in 55 BC, and the first traces of Christianity date back to the influence of Christian Roman soldiers. The Hinton Head of Christ, a Roman mosaic of the fourth century (preserved in the British Museum), and the Roman villa at Lullingstone leave unmistakable evidence of the Christian faith in Britain during the Roman occupation. The bishops of Britain were invited to participate in the Council of Nicaea in 325, but the records of England's spiritual life are missing. The last of the Roman legions left the shores of Britain in 410. The invasion of the Saxons in 449 virtually cut off communication with the rest of the Roman Empire. For hundreds of years the island was in constant turmoil, but records are scanty.

The story goes that nearly 200 years after the Romans left, two fair-haired, blue-eyed boys were being sold in the Roman slave market. Gregory, who later became the Roman pontiff, asked who they were. "They are Angles," was the reply. "Not Angles, but angels," he said. "They ought to be joint-heirs with the angels in heaven." He did not forget these boys when he became Pope. In 596, Gregory commissioned Augustine and forty monks to evangelize Britain. They arrived in Kent the following year, a few months before Columba died in Scotland, and king Ethelbert gave them the use of an old Romano-British church in Canterbury, in which his Christian wife worshipped. Ethelbert and many of his people soon became Christians, Augustine was made

The famous incident when Pope Gregory finds Angles for sale as slaves in Rome.

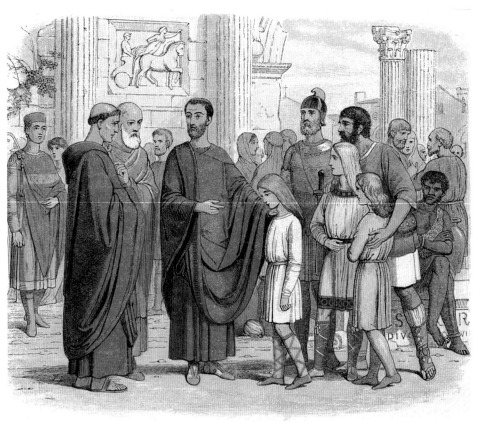

Canterbury Cathedral, Kent.

bishop with power to consecrate other bishops. The mission never reached the entire land, which was splintered into seven kingdoms. Nevertheless it had considerable influence, even reaching as far north as Northumbria, whose king, Edwin, was baptized in York in 627 along with many of his people. To this day, Canterbury is the religious capital of the Church of England.

Seven great men

Here we pause to acknowledge the greatness of seven men who lived in the Anglo-Saxon period. Where the Christian message is written and proclaimed in a dead language, clouded by ritual, it can never satisfy spiritual longings, and these seven men tried, with primitive means, to translate the scriptures into their native tongue. They ranged from a stable hand through to a king.

CÆDMON

Cædmon died in 680. He started off as a servant who worked in the stables at a monastery in Whitby, in the north of England. At first sight, it is strange that he should be listed among Bible translators, because he never translated the scriptures! Yet he did make the Bible available to ordinary men and women, and in a striking and memorable way.

It was the practice for everyone in the monastery to meet in the great hall for a meal at the end of the day. They gathered around a roaring fire and entertained each other by singing with the harp, each one taking turns. Every night, just when it was Cædmon's turn, he would get up and leave, muttering something about the needs of the horses, or the cattle. On one of these nights, while he was pottering in the stable, a "heavenly visitor" came to him, and said, "Cædmon, sing to me!"

He said, "I cannot sing, and for that reason I left the feast."

The voice repeated, "Sing to me."

Cædmon asked, "What shall I sing?"

The visitor said, "Sing of the beginning of created things." Cædmon began, and was amazed at the beauty of the song he was singing, and all he suddenly knew. The next day, the visitor had gone, but the gift remained. The abbess Hilda, seeing the powerful poetic

The Venerable Bede (674–735).

The church at Jarrow, Northumberland, where the Venerable Bede translated John's Gospel.

gift he now possessed, persuaded him to leave secular employment and enter monastic life. A monk would read to him from the Latin Bible, and translate its meaning. Then Cædmon would convert it into poetry, holding his audience spellbound as he sang about the truths of the Bible. Cædmon was one of the earliest poets in England and his songs became a Bible for the people.

ALDHELM AND EGBERT

The next two Bible translators are Aldhelm (c640–709) and Egbert (died 766). Aldhelm, the West Saxon abbot of Malmesbury, translated from the Psalms and bishop Egbert translated from the Gospels.

BEDE

Then came the Venerable Bede (674–735), a monk, scholar, historian and theologian. He wrote a book entitled *The Ecclesiastical History of England*, which earned him the title "Father of English History." He, too, lived in the north of England, in Jarrow. His great and final work was a translation of John's Gospel, which he dictated to a scribe. The scribe was afraid that

Bede's health would break before his task was finished. One morning he saw that Bede was very weak, and said, "Dear master, there is yet one chapter to do, but it seems very hard for you to speak."

"No," responded Bede, "take up your pen and write quickly."

Towards the end of the day, the scribe said, "There is still one verse to finish."

"Write quickly," said the saint. At last he leaned back on his pillow and sighed, "Aye, it is finished!" He then breathed his last, left his frail carcass, and entered into the presence of the One whose message he had spent his last hours translating.

ALFRED

The next Bible translator is the Saxon King Alfred (849–899). During Alfred's reign the Danes were invading the north of England, destroying monasteries and libraries. Alfred struggled to protect his kingdom, eventually securing the southern half of England. His mother was a godly woman from whom Alfred gained a love of books, especially the Bible; and he became a teacher, a writer and a translator of the Scriptures. He translated the Ten Commandments and placed them at the head of his laws for England. He also translated the Psalms, and a portion of the Gospels. His wish was "that all the freeborn youth of his kingdom should employ themselves on nothing till they could first read well the English Scriptures."

The Saxon King Alfred (849–899).

A richly decorated page from the Lindisfarne Gospels.

Whitby Abbey, where Cædmon worked as a stable lad.

ALDRED AND ÆLFRIC

The last two are Aldred and Ælfric, the first a priest of North Northumbria and the second an abbot of Eynsham. They both translated the scriptures during the century or so before the Norman Conquest: Aldred took a manuscript of the Gospels in Latin, and between the lines added a paraphrase in his regional dialect of mid-10th-century Anglo-Saxon. Ælfric, about AD 1000, translated the first seven books of the Old Testament, and the book of Job.

What are these seven men saying to us? A baby cries because it hurts, or it needs something. Rob men and women of the Word of God, and they will search the world to find it. Encode it in a foreign language and they will spend a fortune to break the code. The heart is never satisfied until it is in direct contact with God.

Marriage to the state

It is difficult to tell at what point the decline and fall of the Roman Empire began. The dividing of the Empire between East and West weakened both empires, while the wars against the Goths in 535–553 caused terrible slaughter and devastation in Italy. The situation became even worse with the invasion of the Lombards, another Germanic tribe, in 568–572. The inhabitants of the land became slaves, and little but Rome itself remained unconquered.

A new era began with the accession to the papal chair of Pope Gregory I ("the Great," 540–604), whose brilliant leadership transformed the tragic circumstances he faced. With the wealth acquired by the church, he was able to buy off the Lombard army, who had not been paid their wages. Thus he gave the church the reputation of being the savior of Caesar's realm.

Then in the early 700s a new threat arose, a threat even more terrible than the Goths and Lombards, who were at least nominally Christian. Now the West lived in dread of an Islamic conquest. The Muslims had crossed North Africa and surged up through Spain into southern France, posing a serious threat to all Europe. Had they reached Rome, Europe would have fallen to Islam; but they were defeated by the German ruler Charles Martel in 732.

When the last Lombard king threatened Rome once more, the Pope turned to Charles for help. His victory over the Lombards in 771 extended his domain from Hamburg to Rome. German armies continued to buttress the Empire, and on Christmas Day 800, at St Peter's in Rome, Pope Leo III placed the imperial diadem on the head of Charlemagne, grandson of Charles Martel. (The name is a contraction of Carolus Magnus, meaning "Charles the Great.") From then on, German kings used the title "Kaiser," the German form of the Greek word for Caesar. They called their empire the Holy Roman Empire, though it was neither holy nor Roman, nor even an empire, but merely a union between Germany and northern Italy. At times, however, the Empire claimed control over Poland and Hungary in the east, and in the west over Spain, France, the Scandinavian peninsula and the British Isles. This union gave the pope unprecedented political and military power.

The position of the pope within the Holy Roman Empire swung like a pendulum. At the beginning, pope and emperor ruled as equals over a commonwealth of Europe. In 1024, on the death of the Emperor Otto, the papacy fell under the dominion of the emperor. In 1046, the emperor deposed three popes, and filled the vacant papal chair with his own candidate. Then, in 1075, Pope Gregory VII forbade emperor, king or prince to make any church appointments, even in their own kingdoms. Now the popes started appointing the emperors. Gregory (also called Hildebrand) claimed that the pope stood to the emperor as the sun to the moon. This is well illustrated in the famous story of the pope's excommunication of the emperor Henry IV who, when he repented, was kept standing in the snow, with bare feet, ill-clad, outside the gates of the papal palace at Canossa. The moral of the story is that any union between church and state always ends in the secularization of the church, never in the christianization of the state.

Ignorance was one result of this marriage. The Goths who trampled Italy were little more than savages. It is questionable if even their noblest leaders, including Charlemagne, could either read or write. Hallam, in his book *The Middle Ages*, stated that "in almost every Council the ignorance of the clergy forms a subject for reproach. . . . It was asserted that in one held in 992 scarcely a single person was to be found in Rome itself who knew the first element of letters."

And with ignorance went superstition. Witches, wizards and astrologers had a thriving trade, while fantastic and unbiblical stories were credulously believed. For example, the Virgin Mary was reported to have materialized to support the feet of a man who was being hanged for highway robbery. She sat at his feet until he was taken down and released. She also, it was said, assumed the shape of a nun who had eloped to live a life of sin, working, unsuspected, in the nun's place for ten years until the wayward nun returned to her convent.

Authoritarian control replaced freedom of thought, a control that was easy to enforce in a feudalistic society. Galileo was forced, under threat of torture, to deny his astronomical calculations. When Roger Bacon invented gunpowder, he was afraid to publish the facts, and contented himself with committing its secret to an anagram.

Theology suffered in the union of church and state. No longer God-centered and Spirit-empowered, the church became arid. The big theological discussions of the day concerned subjects like the state of an angel's mind in the morning and evening. The appalling lack of theological content in the pronouncements and councils of the church meant that it was not possible to discuss theological issues with Christians who held divergent views. Groups such as the Albigenses and Waldenses left the church.

In short, the involvement of the church in the politics of that millennium reduced it to a degenerate and apostate machine.

Papacy and tradition

Much of the blame for the darkness of the Middle Ages has to be laid at the door of the church, and especially of the corrupt papacy.

In New Testament times, the Christian minister was known as a "pastor" (a shepherd who fed his flock), an "elder" (the president of a deliberative assembly) or an "overseer" (of a working force; the Greek word is *episcopos* from which we get our word "bishop"). Passages such as Acts 20:17 and 28 show that the three words were synonymous:

"elders" were appointed as "overseers" over a flock they were encouraged to "feed." The Jewish church emphasized the role of the elder, while the Greeks emphasized the role of the bishop or overseer. As time went on, the titles came to be applied to different offices, with the word "bishop" signifying the higher responsibility. At first each church was ruled by a group of overseers/elders, but gradually it became the practice for one "bishop" to lead a church, probably in order to ensure the unity of the church. Where that church was larger and more influential than other churches in the area, often because it was based in the chief town of the area, the bishop of that church became more important.

After the apostles died, and before the Bible canon was agreed upon, the church, as we have seen, was splintered by heresy and strife. Gradually the bishops of Rome assumed wider influence as people in the West looked to Rome for a source of authority. In 440, Leo I gave the official interpretation of Matthew 16; the idea of the "keys," he said, implied apostolic succession. In 607, Boniface III compelled the Emperor to confer the title of "universal bishop" on him. By the twelfth century, Innocent III was exercising secular authority over kings such as John of England. A hundred years later, Boniface VIII was able to say: "The Pope alone is called most holy—divine monarch and supreme emperor and king of kings. . . . Moreover we declare, affirm, define and pronounce that it is necessary to salvation that every human creature be subject to the Roman pontiff."

Pope Boniface VIII, who made high claims for the power of the papacy.

Meanwhile, the importance of tradition in the church was growing. At first there were reports of some teachings of Jesus which had not been committed to writing but handed down through an inner circle of privileged believers. Next came similar reports of what the apostles were supposed to have taught. In the third stage, unpublished letters from respected church fathers were discovered, and added to these oral reports. They were later supported by Council pronouncements and papal decrees, and all of these collectively became a binding tradition. The Word of God, according to the Council of Trent in 1546, was a composite of a written Bible and a handed-down oral tradition.

A ninth-century collection of documents, supposedly provided by someone named Isidore Mercator, strongly supported the supreme authority of the bishop of Rome. Known as the Pseudo-Isidorian Decretals, their origins and authorship are still open to question. A few of the documents were authentic, but they were outnumbered by clever forgeries. Altogether there were ninety-four spurious decretals in the collection, but they were held in great esteem until a voice first questioned them in the fifteenth century. These letters had a very great influence on developing thinking about the papacy.

Attempts had already been made to sort and compile the various decrees of tradition when an Italian Benedictine in the twelfth century, Gratian, made a proper job of classifying and commenting on them. The first part of his collection dealt with legislative issues, the second part with practical applications of the law, and the third part mainly with liturgy. For three centuries virtually no other decrees were referred to but those of Gratian's *Decretals*, and his work became the textbook of all seminaries. By the time the Reformation broke out, most priests graduating from Oxford and Cambridge majored in Canon Law.

It was not the *Decretals* that intensified the darkness in the medieval church, but the unintentional concealing of the sacred Scriptures. Instead of studying the Bible, priests studied canon law; the word of God was hedged in and qualified by the word of tradition; the common people had no Bible in their own everyday language, and were dependent on the ministry of priests who were frequently immoral. All this is what deepened the darkness.

The cross and the crescent

Muhammad was born in Mecca in AD 570. He was a merchant who married a rich widow, and had four daughters by her. He supposedly had visions in which the angel Gabriel communicated to him the Muslim religion, and he became the chief prophet of that religion—which is called "Islam," meaning "submission." It quickly spread into other countries from India to Spain, and today is the second largest religion in the world.

Between 1100 and 1300, the church launched a military campaign against Islam, chiefly in the Middle East. It started when Alexius, the emperor of Constantinople, was threatened by an invasion of Muslim Seljuk Turks, and appealed to the pope for a "Christian army" to assist him. This was of immense interest to western Christians, because the same invaders had taken control of Jerusalem. They were a fanatical and brutal force, and needed to be restrained. At the Synod of Clermont in 1095, Pope Urban II urged the Christian nations to unite and crusade against the heathen. The imagination of western Christendom was fired. Over a million people were involved in this, the first of eight crusades. Some people participated for economic reasons. The West was facing famine, and the Venetians saw the potential of a new market in the East. Some may have responded out of love of military adventure or as an escape either from domestic boredom or criminal punishment. Whatever the reason, the cross was emblazoned on all armor and attached to national flags. It became the emblem of holy war and bloody murder.

Because Urban II, who launched the Crusade movement, was a Frenchman, most of those who responded to the First Crusade were French. A mob of unorganized and undisciplined peasants gathered at Constantinople and set out to meet the foe. They were either massacred or taken prisoner and sold as slaves in Egypt. This caused the nobles of France, Belgium and northern Italy to organize another effort. They also met at

St. Anne's Church, Jerusalem, built by the Crusaders after they captured the Holy City.

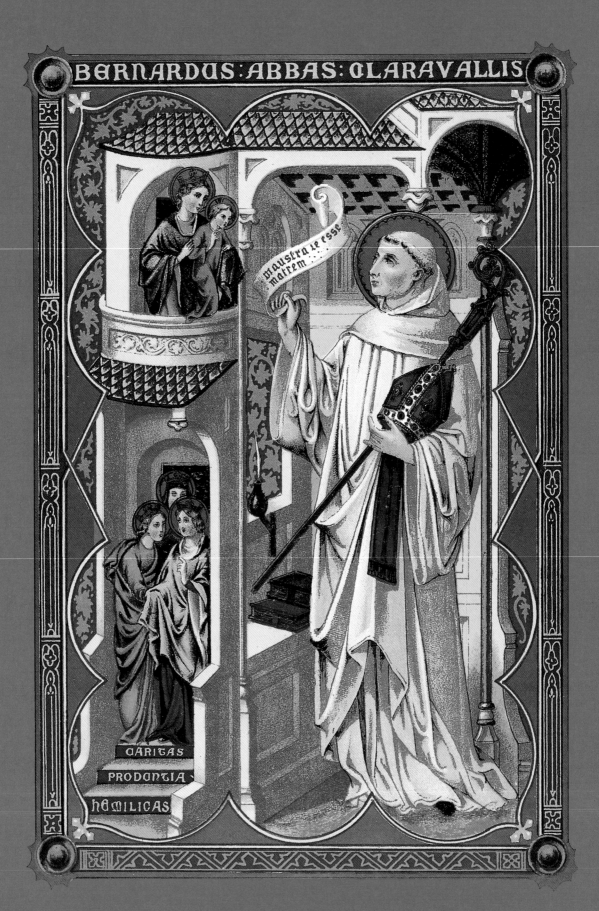

BERNARDUS : ABBAS : CLARAVALLIS

Opposite: Bernard of Clairvaux, whose preaching helped inspire the Second Crusade.

Pope Innocent III, instigator of the Fourth Crusade to the Holy Land.

Constantinople, this time in the spring of 1097; and by June, 1099, they captured Jerusalem. They immediately organized the subjugated province into a Kingdom of Jerusalem, governed on feudal principles.

When the Muslims later threatened their north-eastern flank, they requested a Second Crusade. In 1147 Bernard of Clairvaux preached for another military attack on the Muslims. The King of France and the Holy Roman Emperor united their forces, but the Second Crusade was a failure and Jerusalem was recaptured by Saladin the Muslim in 1187.

The Third Crusade, known as "the King's Crusade," lasted from 1189 to 1192. For the first time England became involved. Richard of England, Philip of France and again the Emperor Frederick, started on this venture. Frederick was accidentally drowned on the way, and Richard and Philip argued with each other, so that Philip returned home, leaving Richard by himself. Although Richard was unable to recapture Jerusalem, he did accomplish the "peace of Saladin," promising future pilgrims access to Jerusalem.

Pope Innocent III considered Egypt to be the key to the problem of the Islamic occupation of the Holy Land. He called for the Fourth Crusade in which he proposed to capture Egypt and use it as a base for future operations against Palestine. The importance of this crusade was that in 1024 the Greek church was made subject to the authority of the pope. This weakened the eastern Empire, and fostered bitterness between Latin and Greek Christians.

The Fifth Crusade was led by Frederick II. In 1229 he succeeded in bringing Jerusalem, Nazareth and Bethlehem, including a corridor to the sea, under the control of the Christians. This was accomplished by a treaty with the Sultan of Egypt, under which the Muslims could retain their Mosque of Omar in the Holy City and Frederick was crowned as the King of Jerusalem. Despite this, there were three more Crusades in the thirteenth century.

The Crusades sank to their lowest depths with the Children's Crusade of 1212, led by two boys named Stephen and Nicholas. The boys believed that their parents' sinfulness had made them lose their battles against the Turks, and assumed that their own pure motives would cause the enemy to fall before them like flies. Children of France and Germany rallied around them and marched across southern Europe and northern Italy. Those who did not perish on the way were sold as slaves in Egypt.

What have these events to do with our English Bible? They all prepared indirectly for the overthrow of church-state control of religion. In England, financing the Crusades impoverished the king and many of his feudal lords, and so contributed to the weakening of the whole feudal system which controlled so many aspects of people's daily lives. (It was during this period that the Magna Carta was signed, conceding that there were limits to the state's power over the individual.) In Europe, the political weakening of Constantinople ultimately led to its collapse in 1453. The scholars and thinkers who had kept classical scholarship alive there fled to the West, bringing their books with them, and we shall see how this gave reformers the tools they needed to understand the Bible. But the immediate result of the Crusades was an increasing resentment of the autocratic demands of the pope.

Cancer surgery

The Albigenses

The Albigenses—who derived their name from Albi, a town with which they were associated—believed that when Satan sinned, God gave him a body and cast him out of heaven. Satan then created this world, with the result that all matter is intrinsically evil. The supreme mission of mankind, they asserted, was to liberate the spirit within from its prison of flesh, a liberation which could only be accomplished by rigorously enforced ascetic restrictions including no marriage, a strict diet, non-participation in war or civil government, and rejection of "objects" in worship. A dying man or woman had to receive the sacrament of "consolamentum"; if not, the spirit was obliged to reincarnate another body.

Few of us would agree with such a creed, but would we defend the right of others to hold to it? In 1119, the Council of Toulouse asked assistance of the secular powers in eradicating this heresy, but the nobles protected the Albigenses and the common people joined them. A hundred years later, when Innocent II occupied the papal chair, he ordered a crusade against these Cathars, as they were also called. It

The fortress-like cathedral at Albi, built to defend the Albigensians from their enemies.

precipitated a war between the princes of the north and the south of France, destroying the independence of the southern nobles. Occasional insurrections occurred, but they were brutally suppressed. Two hundred Cathars were burned to death in one day, and severe reprisals were taken even against those who were sympathetic.

The Waldenses

Peter Waldo, a wealthy merchant, lived in the city of Lyons. In 1173, following a deep religious experience, he determined to distribute his wealth to the poor, keeping only sufficient for his family's survival. Others copied his example and the group became known as the Poor Men of Lyons. The chief tenet of their faith was that the Bible was their supreme authority and Peter Waldo had the Latin New Testament translated into the vernacular. Their faith was orthodox. They believed in the divinity of Jesus, and salvation solely through Christ. Evangelism was the heartbeat of their faith. They believed that church leaders should abandon secular life and live by begging, preferably as celibates, and "preach the Word."

Peter Waldo, founder of the Waldensians.

In 1174 the pope sent missionaries to "convert" the followers of Waldo, or Waldenses as they were called. When persuasion failed, fire, faggot and sword were applied. A Roman Catholic historian, Bzovius, tells of Pope Innocent III's campaign against them, dating from 1206. The pope placed Dominic, founder of the Dominican preaching friars, in charge of the expedition. They captured a camp where they found "180 persons, who preferred being burned alive to adopting a pious creed." In another town "the Lord of Mountroyal was hanged; eighty others, who fell by the gibbet, were slain by the Crusaders . . . and innumerable heretics were burned." In another town, captured in 1215, "450 of them, hardened by the devil, persisted in their obstinacy, of whom 400 were burned, and the rest hanged."

These persecutions, like those upon the Christians of ancient Rome, failed to stamp out the movement. In 1532 the Waldenses joined with the reformers, and became a Protestant denomination. In spite of continuing, often horrific opposition—including a massacre of believers in the Alpine town of Piedmont in 1655—their group continued, and today they number about 20,000.

The Inquisition

The Inquisition, instituted in 1232 on the basis of a program agreed at the Council of Verona in 1184, was the church's official method of purging heresy. It was used wherever Rome held sway. Boettner records that during the reign of three Inquisitors in Spain some 191,285 people died (31,912 of them burned to death). An additional 291,450 suffered imprisonment.

All these barbarisms were perpetrated simply because men and women refused to submit to the official church viewpoint. As the darkness of the Middle Ages dissipated, and men and women began to read the Bible for themselves, the atrocities increased, and then, as we shall see, the Roman Church was not alone in its guilt. But now we move on to the dawning of light and the "Morning Star" of the Reformation.

3. The Bible in England before the Reformation

The dry ground

Isaiah prophesied that the Messiah would "grow up as a root out of a dry ground" (Isaiah 53:2). That may also be said of many reformers who followed their Master, and not least of Wycliffe, England's first great reformer, known as "the Morning Star of the Reformation." Though Wycliffe was not the first man to attack corrupt practices in the church, he was the first to condemn the underlying doctrine. He was born about 1330 in the village of Wycliffe, six miles from Richmond, Yorkshire, but he spent most of his life in Oxford. He was a man of outstanding intelligence, courage and charisma. In a university where the art of arguing was all-important, he could dispute with a panel of the greatest academics and reduce them to silence. When he came to take an unpopular stand on political and religious matters, he stood undaunted before threats from king, Parliament, university and even, most deadly and bitter of all, from the world-wide church. Young men enlisted in his cause and gave their lives to be burned at the stake because they believed he was right.

To appreciate the stature of this man, it is necessary to know something of the "dry ground" of the Middle Ages. The previous chapter has already touched on the religious climate; we now consider two other important aspects of medieval life: language and politics.

Language

The people of Wycliffe's day spoke Middle English, which is basically the same language as modern English, though people today would not understand it if they heard it spoken. The English language passed through three stages. The first was Old English, which began with the tribes who invaded England from the third century onwards. Remember, this is just a small island. Only about 800 miles separate

John O'Groats in the north of Scotland from Land's End at the southernmost tip of England. No place in the island is more than 100 miles from the sea. Foreign marauders repeatedly swept in and took over different parts of the country, bringing their language and culture with them. The Jutes settled in the south-east, the Saxons in the south and the Angles in the middle of Britain, from the Scottish border to the river Thames. The islanders consequently spoke three separate dialects of Old English. The Angles spoke Mercian, a form of which was also spoken in London.

The transition to Middle English came with William the Conqueror, who landed in England only 260 years before Wycliffe was born. His forces spoke Norman French, and this became the language of law and government. But the ordinary people and merchants continued to speak English, though borrowing many words from the French. Modern English, therefore, often has two words for the same thing—for example, the word "lamb," which was used by the serfs, and "mutton," which came from their French masters. The one referred to the animal as it was in the fields, and the other to the meat on the tables.

Two writers of Middle English stand out. Geoffrey Chaucer (c1340–1400) is still regarded as one of the greatest English poets. Everyone knows his masterpiece, the *Canterbury Tales*, but few people are familiar with the great prose writings attributed to Chaucer's friend John Wycliffe.

Politics

In politics there was a similar state of flux. When William the Conqueror took over the island in 1066, he ruled through barons who governed regions for him, collecting taxes and marshaling armies. They grew very powerful, and succeeding kings became dependent on them. Within 150 years they were stubbornly refusing to co-operate with the king without being granted a larger voice in national affairs. King John (who reigned from 1199 to 1216) inherited enormous debts along with his crown, and added further debt by going to war with France. He could receive no assistance from the pope because he had appointed his own Archbishop of Canterbury and rejected the pope's appointee. But he needed money so desperately that he was forced to submit, and even laid his crown at the feet of a papal legate—an act of monumental importance because it subordinated the crown to the miter, the throne to the church.

John could not survive without the financial support of the barons. In return, in 1215 the barons forced him to sign the Magna Carta, which limited the power of the king and recognized the rights of barons, church and freemen. He later attempted to rescind the document, but when he lodged in a monastery in the north of England a monk laced his wine with poison, and the document outlived him. Out of that political conflict came the English Parliament, the forerunner of the American

Congress and many other legislative bodies around the world.

Wycliffe was to play a leading role in directing England out of the political quagmire in which church and state were embroiled, and one of his tools would be the Bible.

The morning star

Of Wycliffe's childhood we know nothing. He spent a number of years in Oxford as an undergraduate—becoming a fellow of Merton College by 1356—and the next sixteen years studying for his doctorate, also at Oxford. In the last twelve years of his life, he kept up his links with Oxford. Though he did some traveling in the service of the crown, Oxford was his base, and here he did most of his teaching and writing: he was truly a citizen of Oxford. He spent the last two years of his life in Lutterworth, where he died in 1384.

What was Oxford like when Wycliffe arrived? When the French evicted all the English students from the University of Paris in 1167, these students had formed their own University in Oxford. The town was hostile to this invasion of robed academics, and a "town and gown" controversy ensued in which opposing sides sometimes came to blows. Consequently, in 1209 some of the students fled to Cambridge, where they founded another university. These two universities quickly became the leading universities of Europe. The year before Wycliffe graduated, sixty-two students were killed by the townspeople in a riot on St Scholastica Day. For the next 468 years, on the same day, the townspeople placed sixty-two pennies on the altar at St Mary's to atone for that misdeed.

When Wycliffe was a student, the dreaded Black Death arrived in England. It was merciless, touching both rich and poor, young and old. The people of London used the open acres of ground at Smithfield as a common burial site, and soon they were burying 200 victims a day. This continued until the plague had claimed over 100,000 lives.

During this terrifying plague, Wycliffe experienced a profound spiritual revival that reached to the core of his being. The holy fear of God that came upon him brought a disregard for human popes and potentates: it seemed that he held communion with the citizens of the invisible world. He rearranged his priorities and became more earnest in his theological studies. The transformation was soul-shattering and proved to be permanent.

In 1356 he graduated from Merton College. Five years later, in 1361, he added his Master of Arts, and eight years later, in 1369, when he was in his forties, he was awarded his Bachelor of Divinity degree. Then in 1372 he earned his doctorate in divinity. By this time he was already considered the outstanding philosopher and theologian of Oxford, which means he was probably the most prominent theologian of

England. He was the leading speaker at theological debates, and when he lectured his classrooms were always crowded.

In 1361 he was ordained for the ministry and accepted a living at Fillingham in Lincolnshire, which maintained him until he was appointed to the rectory of Lutterworth. He did not live in either of these places, however, except when he retired to Lutterworth at the end of his life, for neither was within commuting distance of Oxford and his first love was teaching. (It was acceptable practice, in those days, to have "absentee parsons," but it was the parson's responsibility to find someone to take his place in the parish.) Wycliffe's debates in Oxford sharpened his convictions and his studies led him to value truth above tradition. The longer he studied, the more he saw issues in terms of truth or falsehood, black or white. He could see clearly where there was wrong thinking and evil practice, even when they were robed in the red and purple garments of a high-ranking clergyman. Whether the issues were sacred or secular, political or ecclesiastical,

Right was right and wrong was wrong, and right the day must win.
To doubt would be disloyalty, to falter would be sin.

In Oxford, Wycliffe the fighter was born, and his sword was, above all, the Bible.

The Cold War

During this time Rome and Oxford were engaged in a cold war, fighting a battle on two fronts.

The political front

In Wycliffe's day nearly all the leading positions of state were occupied by the clergy, who were influential and aggressive. This state of affairs was wrong. It harmed the clergy, who were called to a superior ministry, and it was damaging for the state, since these men took their orders from Rome. Quite simply, it was bad politics.

In addition, major religious positions were filled by the pope's nominees, many of whom were foreigners, who never even set foot on English soil but had their lucrative salaries sent to them. While Wycliffe could see the political harm of this policy, he felt the religious harm more keenly. Clergymen were being bought, sold and traded in return for favors to their religious superiors, and any sense of sacred service to Christ had vanished from their pulpits. Wycliffe wrote a tract on this subject before Parliament presented a petition to the king concerning the grip which Rome had on England. Most students of history are persuaded that it was Wycliffe who gave Parliament the ammunition and the incentive for its action.

The highest insult to England came when French priests were

John Wycliffe (c1330–84).

awarded positions in the church in England. This was a foolish move on the part of Rome. England at that time was engaged on the Hundred Years War against France, and these appointments only inflamed passions and aggravated hostilities. This was the final straw and it provoked the English Parliament to pass two very important statutes.

The first was the Statute of Provisors, in 1351. This stated that no one had the right to make any appointment on foreign soil when that appointment could be considered an insult to the sovereign of the country. The statute ruled that foreign appointments within the English realm must first receive the king's approval.

The second was the Statute of Praemunire, passed in 1353. This law prevented any foreign court from demanding trial, or exacting penalty from any Englishman, before he had been tried in an English court. It also nullified any existing writ demanding that an Englishman appear for trial in a foreign country. In future such writs would require the permission of Parliament.

These statutes were soon to be tested. When King John had placed his crown before a papal legate (see previous section), Pope Innocent III had imposed an annual tax of £666 on the British crown. It was paid, erratically, until 1320. In 1365, the pope demanded the reinstatement of this tax, and an immediate payment of the arrears. To add insult to injury, the following year a papal Bull was issued ordering the king to appear in Rome and defend himself. Those decisions on Rome's part trampled over Parliament's Statute of Praemunire.

Six years later, in 1372, the year Wycliffe received his doctorate, Rome sent an agent to collect money for the pope's war with Milan. The agent's extravagant and pompous retinue, his costly robes, and his large staff of accountants requiring numerous rooms, were all more suitable for a minister of state than a representative of the church. The pope's emissary promised Parliament that he would do nothing that was against the interests of the king, but Wycliffe could see that he was promising what he could not perform. Immediately Wycliffe published a tract pointing out that the nature of the agent's mission was inconsistent with his promise to Parliament, which, in effect, made him a liar.

Two years later, Wycliffe was appointed to a royal commission which was sent to Bruges in an attempt to relieve tension between London and Rome. That assignment occupied the next two years of his life but proved to be a tedious waste of time. Many of the English bishops on the commission gave way when their foreign superiors promised them lucrative jobs, but Wycliffe could not be bribed or swayed, and resolutely opposed payment of the tribute. Though he failed to turn the negotiations, his stance endeared him to Parliament and earned him the friendship of John of Gaunt, the powerful fourth son of the king. Wycliffe was later made a royal chaplain.

The theological front

The second front in the cold war centered on Wycliffe's rejection of the doctrine of transubstantiation. This doctrine, a recent innovation, dating only to 1215, attempted to explain the words of Jesus, "This is my body." The church contended that though the "accidents" or "species" (the bread and wine observable by human senses) remained the same, their substance was literally and mysteriously changed into the actual body and blood of Christ. Wycliffe saw serious problems in this interpretation, which he considered to be unscriptural. The fact that he had received his doctorate in 1372 suggests that he was not considered heretical by the church at that time, but after he published his book *On the Eucharist* in 1381 he lost most of his friends in palace, Parliament and university.

The pen is mightier

Wycliffe gave lectures to his students on the secular immoralities of the church. But he decided that his pen was more powerful than his pulpit. There were no printing presses and all publications had to be hand

Lutterworth Parish church, where John Wycliffe, who instigated the translation of the Bible into English, was rector.

written, and then painstakingly hand-copied for distribution; but the pen was nevertheless the most potent vehicle for the dissemination of revolutionary ideas.

Wycliffe's earliest writing was a tract written in 1360 entitled it *Objections to Friars*, in which he accused the friars of disrupting school discipline and domestic relationships, and called them a pestilence. He said they were guilty of ignorance and proselytizing, and were a major inconvenience both to church and to university. Two important facts about this tract deserve notice. First, it was not an attack on the church but on a corrupt order of friars within it. Second, it gained Wycliffe great support in the University of Oxford.

His great treatise on *Civil Dominion*, written in 1376, was aggressive and strong. He declared that "England belongs to no pope. The pope is but a man, subject to sin; but Christ is the Lord of lords, and this kingdom is held directly and solely of Christ alone." John Wycliffe considered that the division between Rome and London was irreconcilable and went so far as to argue that "every papal resident in England, and every Englishman living at the court of Rome, should be punished with death."

In 1378 he wrote *The Truth of Holy Scripture* in which he made clear his view on truth in the Bible. He stated that the scriptures are without error and contain God's entire revelation. No further teaching from any other source is necessary, and all other teaching must be tested against the Bible.

His book *On the Eucharist*, published in 1381, was followed by *Twelve Propositions*. As we have seen, his courageous stance against what he regarded as unbiblical teaching lost him the friendship and support of much of the establishment.

In Wycliffe's writings we see all the seeds of the Reformation. For nearly every issue on which he expressed his opinion, godly men were burned at the stake 150 years later. He condemned trust in personal works, pardons, indulgences and priestly absolution. He called the sale of indulgences "a subtle merchandise of Antichrist's clerks to magnify their counterfeit power, and to get worldly goods, and to cause men to dread sin." He held that Scripture comes "from the mouth of God": it is the truth—superior to the teaching of the pope, the Church or the Fathers, and tells us all we need to know. Wycliffe set the table and wrote the menu for the great reform that was to shake Europe to its roots.

One of his last tracts was the *Trialogue* which took the form of a conversation between Truth, Falsehood and Understanding. "The church has fallen," he argued, "because she has abandoned the gospel and preferred the laws of the pope. Although there should be a hundred popes in the world at once [there were two contending at the time], and all the friars living should be transformed into cardinals, we must withhold our confidence from them in the matter of faith, except so far as their teachings are those of the Scriptures."

Wycliffe's powerful and prolific pen was dipped in acid. But its greatest product was yet to come—a Bible in the language of the ordinary Englishman and woman (see the next section). However, he had first to face the fury of an offended church.

The lion's den

After Wycliffe wrote *Civil Dominion*, the opposition determined that, by one means or another, Wycliffe must be silenced. The threats now turned into action.

On February 19, 1377, Wycliffe was called to answer charges before a convocation of bishops at St Paul's. The trial drew a fanatical crowd, blindly obedient to the church. When Wycliffe arrived, it was with a small procession of men who supported and helped him. These included the two most powerful men in England: Lord Percy, the marshal of England, and John of Gaunt, the Duke of Lancaster, who was administering the kingdom during the terminal sickness of Edward III. These two great men walked ahead of Wycliffe. Following him were four doctors of divinity, who were his counsel. They bravely threaded their way through the hostile crowds thronging the entrances to the church. Once they stepped across the threshold, they were confronted by a solid wall of booing people, who swayed to and fro, their hands raised in anger. The prince turned to Wycliffe and assured him that they were there to protect him. Some sharp, angry words passed between Percy and Courtenay, the Bishop of London. When Percy noticed that Wycliffe

stood during this exchange, he turned to him and said, "Sit down and rest yourself." This assumption of authority enraged Courtenay, who was acting as chairman, and he cried, "It is unreasonable that one cited to appear before a bishop should sit down during his answer. He must and shall stand." A riot broke out which disrupted the entire proceedings, and Wycliffe and his escort providentially escaped from the threatening danger.

Later that year five papal Bulls were issued against Wycliffe, the Benedictines having examined his writings and taken exception to eighteen propositions, and King Edward III was ordered to place Wycliffe in prison awaiting the pope's pleasure. The king, however, was a sick man, on the point of death, and no action was taken against Wycliffe.

Early in 1378, with the new Richard II a mere boy of ten, Wycliffe appeared once more before the bishops. The citation was issued by the Archbishop of Canterbury; the king and the university were silent. The venue was astutely changed from St Paul's to Lambeth Palace, the London residence of the Archbishop of Canterbury. Again there were angry crowds. "Men expected that he should be devoured," wrote one historian, "being brought into the lion's den." But there was uneasiness at the royal palace. As we have seen, a law had been passed stating that papal Bulls should have no effect in England without the consent of Parliament and

Balliol College, Oxford, where John Wycliffe was Master from 1360.

king. Shortly after the trial began, it was interrupted by Sir Louis Clifford with a message from the old king's widow to the effect that they should pass no verdict on the Reformer. The bishops were panic-stricken. They made an immediate about-turn, attempted to placate Wycliffe, and told him simply that he should not argue his controversial opinions in Oxford university or preach them from the pulpit.

In the winter of 1380–1381, a commission of twelve Oxford doctors investigated Wycliffe's teaching on the Mass and concluded, by a majority of seven to five, that Wycliffe was in error. The chancellor warned that anyone who held such views, taught them or defended them would be imprisoned, suspended from university office and excommunicated. In response, Wycliffe declared that the chancellor could not possibly make him weaken his opinion; and in May 1381 he published a defense of the condemned opinions.

This was the year of the Peasants' Revolt, when, under the leadership of Wat Tyler and John Ball, peasants marched on London to air their grievances, and the King was obliged to seek refuge in the Tower of London. Those in authority suggested that Wycliffe's views had inspired the revolt, and in 1382 a Council of theologians meeting at Blackfriars in London decreed that his writings contained both heresy and error. In the middle of their proceedings, an earthquake shook the whole building, whereupon both the supporters of Wycliffe and his detractors claimed that it showed God agreed with them. Wycliffe's enemies instigated a Parliamentary bill condemning Wycliffe's teachings and this bill was given royal assent without ever being debated by the Commons.

The attack was now concentrated on Wycliffe's Oxford disciples, many of whom were brought to recant publicly. Wycliffe himself, who had not been present at Blackfriars, escaped such a fate. In 1382 he left Oxford and retired to Lutterworth, where he continued to write despite the effects of a stroke. On December 28, 1384, while he was at communion in his parish church, he suffered a second stroke and slumped back into his chair. Four men came forward, lifted up the chair and carried it silently out through a side door of the church to the parsonage. The old man never spoke another word until he talked with his Savior in the presence of the angels on the last day of that year.

A book for burning

Before Wycliffe, others had translated parts of the Bible into English. We have already looked at the work of the "seven great men" (see previous chapter). In addition, about the year 1200, Orm, an Augustinian monk, made a metrical paraphrase of parts of the Gospels. He was followed by William of Shoreham, a parish priest living in Kent, who made a translation of the Psalms in 1320. A third translator was Richard Rolle, a hermit from Yorkshire, who in 1340 also made a translation of the Psalms, adding a verse by verse commentary. But it was left to Wycliffe and his followers to provide the first complete Bible in the English language. Wycliffe fervently believed that the Bible needed no special interpretation even for laymen to understand, but since the ordinary man could not understand Latin, the Bible had to be translated into English.

Wycliffe's Bible was not a translation from the original languages, for two reasons: first, the manuscripts which later became available had not yet been discovered, and second, Hebrew and Greek were little known

Painting of John Wycliffe from Balliol College.

A page from the Wycliffe Bible.

in England. But Wycliffe and his followers were good Latin scholars, and the source for their translation of the Scriptures was Jerome's Vulgate of AD 405. As the church accepted the authority of the apocryphal writings, the Wycliffe Bible included them.

It is not clear whether or not Wycliffe himself did any of the translation but he certainly inspired, instigated and probably supervised the work. There is every reason to believe that the Old Testament, as far as Baruch 3:20, was translated by (or under the direction of) Nicholas Hereford, one of Wycliffe's disciples and fellow workers. There is a sharp contrast between the style of the translation before and after that point. The first part was scholarly, stiff and excessively literal—it may have been intended chiefly as a "crib" for those clergy who needed help with following their Latin Bibles—whereas the remainder inclined more to the common language of the people. We know that Nicholas Hereford was summoned to stand trial in London as a heretic, and was excommunicated from the church. We do not know for certain who was responsible for the rest of the translation, but tradition has it that Wycliffe worked on some or all of the New Testament.

That was *the* Bible in English until, in 1396, a dozen years after Wycliffe's death, a revision was made by John Purvey, who had been Wycliffe's close assistant and secretary during the Reformer's retirement at Lutterworth. Purvey revised the literal, crabbed style of the original Old Testament translation to make it much more readable and in keeping with the style of the New Testament. It is Purvey's revision that was circulated as the Wycliffe Bible, and it is impossible to over-emphasise its importance and influence.

Remember, there were as yet no printing presses. It took ten months to reproduce one copy of the Bible, and the cost of a copy was between £30 and £40. It was reported that two pennies could buy a chicken, and four a hog. £40 was 9,600 pennies—an enormous amount of money. Fox wrote of people who provided a load of hay for the privilege of having the New Testament to read *for one day*. Some would save for a month in order to purchase a single page. Soon copies had to be made and distributed by stealth, the Arundel Constitutions of 1408 having decreed that "no one henceforth do by his own authority translate any text of Holy Scripture into the English tongue or into any other, by way of book or treatise; nor let any book or treatise now lately composed in the time of John Wycliffe, or since, or hereafter be composed, be read in whole or in part, in public or private, under pain of the greater excommunication. ... He that shall do contrary to this shall likewise be punished as a favorer of heresy and error." The "punishment" referred to involved execution by burning. Nevertheless, so many copies were produced that even today there still exist over 200 manuscript copies of this Bible. Wycliffe had started something in England which it was impossible to stop. He had released an irresistible force that would dispel the darkness, liberate the church and elevate the social conditions of mankind for generations to come.

No man is an island

By the time of Wycliffe's death, his disciples, or Lollards, looked upon themselves as a Christian church, dependent on the Bible, and independent of Rome. They accepted the priesthood of all believers and administration of the sacraments by men who had not been ordained by a bishop. The poverty of the Wycliffites, and their insistence on preaching in the language of the people rather than in Latin, won them respect. Their views were so popular that Wycliffite slogans and insults were placarded on the walls of St Paul's and other public places. In 1395 a manifesto was nailed to the door at Westminster Hall demanding that Parliament "abolish celibacy, transubstantiation, prayers for the dead, offerings at images, auricular confession, the practice of blessing the oil," and so on.

When Wycliffe's supporters nailed the *Twelve Conclusions*, a summary of the teaching of the early Lollards, on to the doors of St Paul's and Westminster Abbey, Arundel, the Archbishop of York, and Braybrooke, the Bishop of London, reacted angrily, storming off to King Richard II, who was in Ireland at the time. By then the king's wife, Anne of Bohemia, had died, and without her influence for good, the king was easily swayed by these men. When he returned to England, he ordered Parliament not to deliberate the issue, threatening to punish anyone who persisted in defending the followers of Wycliffe. A strange twist of circumstances then occurred. Richard had previously quarreled violently with his cousin, Henry Bolingbroke, the son of Wycliffe's patron John of Gaunt, and had banished Bolingbroke from the country. When Richard was in Ireland, Bolingbroke had landed in Yorkshire and amassed a rebel army. His efforts were a success. In 1399, he dethroned Richard and became England's new king, Henry IV.

Thomas Arundel, now Archbishop of Canterbury, had seen the handwriting on the wall and had already deserted Richard to align with Henry. It was he who placed the crown on the head of Henry, and directed him at the coronation to "consolidate the throne, conciliate the clergy and sacrifice the Lollards." Henry replied, "I will be the protector of the church." Two years later, in 1401, the infamous *De Haeretico Comburendo*, the Act for burning heretics, was passed by Parliament. Within eight days of its passage, the fires of Smithfield were burning for William Sawtre, the first martyr for Wycliffe's doctrine, who had been guilty of saying, "Instead of adoring the cross on which Christ suffered, I adore Christ who suffered on it." He was dragged to the precincts of St Paul's cathedral, where his head was ceremonially shaved. A layman's cap was put on his head and then he was handed over to the "mercy" of the state.

Lambeth Palace, London seat of the Archbishop of Canterbury.

With Lollardy condemned in the Constitutions of Arundel (see the previous section), a Lollards' prison was built at Lambeth Palace, the London residence of the Archbishop of Canterbury. It was a room twelve feet by twelve, with a ceiling seven feet high; it is still there, with iron rings attached to the wall a few feet apart. You can still see the etchings made on the wall by the prisoners. One reads "Jesus amor meus" (Jesus is my love).

In Norwich, the Bishop was zealous in his persecution of the Lollards, causing so many to be killed that the place of public execution became known as the Lollards' Pit. Such burnings took place all over England, testifying to the large numbers of Lollards who were willing to die for their faith.

The faith of these persecuted people is exemplified by Sir John Oldcastle who took the title of Lord Cobham through his third wife. He became a disciple of Wycliffe's theology, attended the preaching of Lollard priests, and helped to provide literature in English for them to distribute. He was brought to trial at St Paul's on September 23, 1413. When he was questioned, and the shouting priests demanded, "Believe!" Sir John responded: "I am willing to believe all that God desires, but that the pope should have authority to teach what is contrary to Scripture—that I can never believe." At this he was led back to the Tower of London. Two days later he was attacked in the most abusive language by the priests, canons, friars and indulgence-sellers, but he was adamant. He informed them: "I ask not for your absolution: it is God's only that I need."

He was given forty days to prepare his soul for death in the hope that he would recant before his execution, and so weaken the Lollard cause. Miraculously he escaped from the Tower, and fled to Wales, where he led a Lollard rising. After three years, he was recaptured, in December of 1417, and dragged on a hurdle to St Giles's Fields, tied by chains to a spit over a slow fire, and slowly roasted to death like a hog.

Wycliffe's followers could not be stamped out by persecution. They were still numerous and active 125 years later, when the Reformation started in earnest and turned all Europe upside down.

The priest of Prague

The fires of reform that were being kindled in England were burning also in Bohemia (today part of the Czech republic). In 1360 the king of Bohemia invited Conrad of Waldhausen to come and preach against the corruption which was prevalent in the church. That was the beginning of a national reform movement which was later to focus in a man called John Huss.

Born in 1372, Huss entered an elementary school when he was twelve. Five years later he enrolled as a student at the University of Prague, where he remained as student and professor for the rest of his life. He earned his B.A. and his M.A. degrees in 1396 and was then

Sir John Oldcastle (Lord Cobham), a Wycliffite who was burned for his faith.

An ancient engraving of the murder of a Wycliffite, Richard Hunne, in what became known as the Lollards' Tower, in the Tower of London.

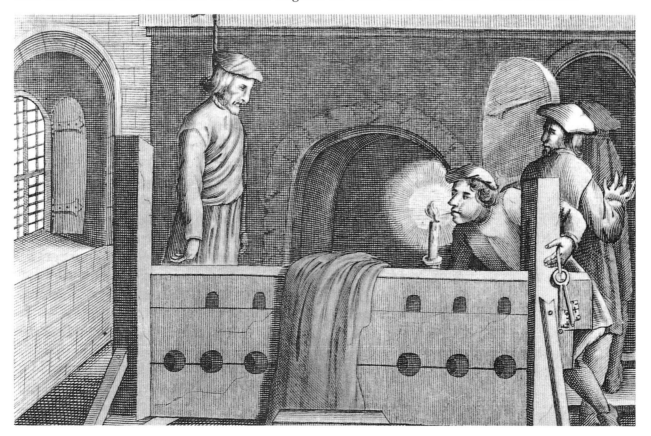

invited to teach on the faculty. He used this opportunity to pursue a bachelor's degree in theology, which he gained in 1404. By then he had become a prominent leader in the reform movement.

In 1400 he was ordained as a priest, and two years later he was appointed to the key position of rector and preacher at the Bethlehem Chapel in Prague. The chapel had been founded by a wealthy merchant as a center of the reformed movement, and two sermons were delivered there daily. Into this environment came the explosive ideas of John Wycliffe.

The Wycliffe connection came through a Bohemian princess, Anne, who, in 1382, had married Richard II of England. In England Anne came across Wycliffe's writings and became an ardent supporter of his teaching. Not only was she able to sway the king's thinking, but she brought an entourage of ladies-in-waiting who exerted considerable spiritual influence over the court in England. The presence of a Bohemian queen in the courts of Richard led several students to come over from Bohemia to study in England. One of these students returned to Prague with several of the more reformed writings of Wycliffe. When Anne died in 1394, her bereaved ladies-in-waiting returned to Bohemia with the writings of Wycliffe in their traveling bags. These were distributed throughout the state of Bohemia.

Though Huss did not agree with Wycliffe's views on transubstantiation, he did accept several of Wycliffe's propositions, notably Wycliffe's denial of the need for popes, priests and prelates, and his support for the participation of the laity in the cup of the communion, an idea which was totally unacceptable to Rome.

There were a large number of Germans in Prague, with power to vote, and as a result of their influence the University condemned Wycliffe on forty-five issues. This divided the entire country, and led the king to eliminate the German vote at the University. At this, the Germans packed their bags and quit Prague, leaving Huss with supreme influence over the city and its university.

The Church of Rome was furious, and in February 1411 the archbishop obtained a papal ban on all preaching at the Bethlehem Chapel. Huss refused to obey, so he was excommunicated. The archbishop burned 200 volumes of Wycliffe's writings, and Huss responded by publicly defending Wycliffe. For this he was ordered to go to Rome and respond to questions. Once more, he refused to comply with the pope's orders.

In 1412, Pope John XXIII launched a crusade against the King of Naples and offered all the supporting soldiers full remission of sins in return for their assistance. Huss was so outraged at such unwarranted spiritual concessions that he more openly attacked the entire idea of the sale of indulgences. The result was that the city of Prague was placed under interdict by the pope, which meant that no religious services

could be conducted, not even baptisms or funerals. Under this pressure, Huss left the city and went into southern Bohemia, spending his time in writing two important books, one on the church and the other on the buying and selling of positions in the church.

During this time three contesting popes were simultaneously attempting to rule the Church: Gregory XII in Rome, Benedict XIII in Perpignan and John XXIII in Avignon, France. They had been condemning and anathematizing each other and so dividing the power of the church. In 1414–1418 a Council was convened in the Swiss city of Constance, in the hope that the schism might be resolved and the papacy reunited. The emperor, Sigismund, wanted to resolve the Huss/Wycliffe issue at the same time, and invited Huss to Constance, promising safe passage in both directions, no matter what the outcome of the dispute might be. With great hesitation Huss accepted the emperor's offer. The Council did mend the papal schism, but behaved treacherously to Huss.

Within a month of his arrival, he was captured on orders from the popes, and put in prison, awaiting trial for heresy. When the Bohemians heard about it, they protested vehemently, but the popes maintained that the arrest was in keeping with canon law and to deceive heretics was a pious act. After languishing in prison for eight months without a trial, Huss was taken from his dungeon to the cathedral in Constance. On July 6, 1415, he was publicly disgraced by the removal of every article of priestly clothing, each with a curse. Then he was made to wear a conical cap with an inscription identifying him as a heretic. At the city gates, tied with water-soaked ropes, he was burned to death. His martyrdom became the symbol of the reformed movement.

Candles in the darkness

If we were to delineate the Middle Ages politically, they would begin at the fall of Rome in 476 and reach to the discovery of America in 1492. In terms of religion, the period stretches from the conversion of Constantine in 312 to Erasmus' Greek New Testament in 1516. Looked at from the point of view of scholarship, the Middle Ages begin with the fall of Rome, and end some time after the fall of Constantinople in 1453, and the development of the printing press in 1454. Within this period we may distinguish between the "Dark Ages" of the earlier part and the revival of learning in the later part. This revolution in academic attitudes came about in three stages.

Scholasticism
When all the secular schools of the Roman empire were swept away by the barbarian hordes, the only institution left was the church. In 800 Charlemagne became the emperor and he gradually established cathedral schools for the training of priests, and convent schools for the training of monks. He also had a palace school for his own children and the children of his nobles, and often studied with them. He ordered manuscripts, especially manuscripts of the Bible, to be copied with extreme care, and it became axiomatic that the church was the guardian of education. Knowledge increased and minds began to open. Though theology was the only subject of study, the approach was philosophical. Attempts were made to reduce Christian doctrine to scientific form, and to harmonize reason and religion. Because the teachers were known as schoolmen, or scholastics, this movement, which flourished from the eleventh to the fourteenth centuries, became known as scholasticism. Some of the discussions were trifling and absurd and scholasticism

came under severe criticism from Roger Bacon, who died some thirty years before Wycliffe was born. In fact, Wycliffe was considered the last of the scholastics.

Humanism

The second stage came with Francesco Petrarch, an Italian poet who was contemporary with John Wycliffe. He studied art, society and especially literature, focusing attention on human achievement. Under his influence, scholasticism gave way to humanism and the foundation was laid for an age of "inner motivated" men who emphasised human values and rational thought and studied the liberal arts, such as history, poetry, philology and rhetoric. This stage reached its peak at the beginning of the sixteenth century with such scholars as John Colet, Thomas More, and Erasmus.

ANCISCVS · PETRARCH

Francesco Petrarch, the Italian poet and humanist.

The Renaissance

The third stage came with the fall of Constantinople in 1453. The ancient city of Byzantium, which Constantine had enlarged and renamed, became, in AD 330, the seat of government for the whole Roman Empire. It survived for more than eleven centuries before falling to the Turks, who made it the capital of their Ottoman Empire. At its fall, the Greeks fled from Constantinople to the west, taking with them their humanist scholarship and culture. The mixing of eastern and western cultures brought about a renaissance of learning in western Europe which affected many fields of endeavor. In fine art, when Raphael or Leonardo da Vinci put paint on canvas, they expressed the humanism that had captured the minds of Europe. They painted people, even nudes, with a new care for accuracy of representation. Michelangelo's sculpture showed the same interest in the human body. In architecture, builders became imaginative and inventive, introducing new ideas in space, decoration and style. The dome was brought from the east and began to be seen on many western buildings.

The new appreciation of art of all kinds spread to music. Musicians and composers were esteemed as important people in their own right, and there was a resurgence of creativity. Music was also secularised. Composers turned to poets for lyrics and the madrigal was born.

In the field of scholarship, there was a rebirth of what is called classical education. Scholars not only explored new subjects, but also adopted new tools, such as the classical language of Greek. This led to a study of Greek and Latin authors, and required the collecting, printing, annotating and translating of the writings of the great thinkers of Greece and Rome.

The exploration of new concepts and the intellectual interest in Greek led to an interest in the original text of the New Testament. Study of the New Testament in Greek was no longer frowned upon, since it

Opposite: Johann Gutenberg, who printed the first Bible.

was associated with a revival in learning. The day had dawned on the dark medieval night.

The end of ignorance

Johann Gutenberg

About the time that Constantinople fell, the process began for the publication of the first printed Bible. It came to fruition some three years later, on August 15, 1456. Its printer, Johann Gutenberg, was a visionary of the type who has millions of dollars in the bank but cannot afford the cab fare to get there and collect it.

Johann was born in Mainz, Germany, about 1398. His father, Friele zum Gensfleisch, was a well-to-do gentleman and one of the city's leading officials. (Gutenberg took his name from the place of his mother's birth.) How his father made his fortune is not known to us. Some historians relate that he was a scribe who carefully copied manuscripts, and it was that tedious and tiring work that motivated his son to invent the printing press. We have no doubt that the father lost his fortunes— Johann's later financial calamities prove it—and it is surmised that he lost them at the uprisings of the artisans in 1428. The family was finally forced to leave Mainz in 1434 and for the next ten years they lived in Strasbourg. While at Strasbourg, Johann seized and imprisoned the town clerk of Mainz for a debt owed to him by the corporation of that city. But when the mayor and the councilors of Strasbourg disapproved of his conduct, he withdrew his charges and forfeited all claims to the money.

The story is told that as a boy Johann entertained himself in his father's workshop by carving the separate letters of his name on soft wood. He was lining them up on his father's table when the "H" fell off into a bucket of purple dye. He quickly retrieved it, cleaned off the excess on the side of the bucket, and let it rest on a piece of paper to dry. The impression it left on the paper, and in his mind, was indelible. This was where the concept of a printing press with movable type was born. If this story is true, it took some forty years for the press to move from an idea to a reality.

Gutenberg eventually produced a steel stamp, or punch, of each letter of the alphabet, which, when stamped into a block of the softer metal, copper, created a mold or matrix into which hot metal could be poured, and any amount of type cast. But this process was expensive: it involved not only the manufacture of type and the building of presses, but also the creation of special printing inks. The paper of that day, made from rags, was also expensive. Gutenberg was to print 200 copies of the Bible on paper. Each page had two columns of 42 lines, and each Bible had a total of 1,282 pages. He was also to produce 30 of his Bibles on vellum,

An artist's impression of the English printer William Caxton showing proofs to visitors.

made from the hides of calves; and it required 10,000 calves just to accomplish this task. All this required money, and it was money he did not have. He had to find it.

In 1450, a lawyer by the name of Johann Fust advanced 800 guilders to Gutenberg to promote his work, requiring no other security than the tools which were to be made by the investment. Fust was also to have provided 300 guilders every year for expenses, though there is no record that this ever happened. In 1452, Fust had to come up with another 800 guilders, in order to prevent the collapse of Gutenberg's entire venture. Some time before November 1455 Fust took legal proceedings against Gutenberg, apparently won the case, and moved all the tools to his own house in Mainz. There, with the assistance of Peter Schoeffer, they published various books. It is not known if the Bible had been printed before the court case. If it had, all the money that came from its sale would have undoubtedly gone to Fust.

Johann Gutenberg died in Mainz in 1468, destitute and forgotten. He was buried in the Franciscan church, but it was demolished and replaced by another church, which in turn has also been demolished. It is tragic how simple it was to erase the knowledge of a man who had created a machine which did so much to bring about the sudden death of medieval ignorance.

Some thirty years later, his invention had been reproduced in nearly every country in Europe. By 1500, there were no fewer than 151 printing shops in Venice alone; and in the town of Wittenberg, Luther's city, a printer by the name of Lufft produced more than 100,000 Bibles. Because the paper contained no wood, the pages have remained white to this day, and the gold of the illuminated initials has lost none of its splendor.

William Caxton

William Caxton was the first English printer. He had been an apprentice to Robert Large, the Lord Mayor of London, upon whose death he was sent to Bruges, where he was responsible for the central foreign market of the Anglo-Flemish trade. He later became the commercial adviser to Margaret, Duchess of Burgundy. By July 1471, he was in Cologne, where he learned the art of printing. In 1476 when he returned to England, he set up a printing press "at the sign of the Red Pale" in Westminster. He published about a hundred volumes, printing over 18,000 pages, and although he did not print the Bible, his presses fired the imagination of English reformers. Burning in their minds was a new idea: a printed English Bible.

A carving of Erasmus, from his birthplace museum.

Playing with matches

A child came into the world in 1466 or 1467, born (like his brother Peter) the illegitimate son of a monk. The parents later married, and the father named the boy Herasmus. Later, Herasmus decided to adopt the Greek form of his name, Erasmus, preceding it with the Latin equivalent, Desiderius, and, because he was born in Rotterdam, he added Roterodamus. Desiderius Erasmus Roterodamus became known to the world as Erasmus, one of the keenest brains of the humanist movement.

At the age of eight he went to the School of the Brethren of the Common Life, attached to St Lebuins' church in Deventer, where he made important acquaintances, including Adrian of Utrecht, who became pope during the great Lutheran debate.

At the age of eleven, he suffered a very great tragedy when first his mother and then his father died of the plague. Though custodians for his welfare were named, one of them soon died of the same plague. In that day, defenseless and immature children were kidnapped by monks or enticed into religious orders. His brother Peter submitted to the enticements of the monks, but Erasmus refused. His health was weak and he felt he would be unable to stand the rigors of monastic life. Moreover, he was a free spirit and did not want to be in bondage to any person or power on earth. He did, however, agree to a friend's suggestion that he become a boarder in an Augustinian monastery for a three-month trial period. This gave him access to the library and required no fasting.

At the end of the three months, facing the prospect of being homeless and penniless, Erasmus had little choice but to take the next step and

The Erasmus birthplace, Rotterdam, now a museum in his honor.

become a novice. This led, in 1486, to his reluctantly becoming an Augustinian canon. He was ordained in 1492, but left the monastery a few years later, and took up the position of Latin secretary to the Bishop of Cambrai. Thus ends the first chapter of his life.

The second chapter opened when an old schoolmaster persuaded the Bishop to let Erasmus study at the University of Paris. Poems he had written were already circulating in Paris, and he was welcomed there by the intelligentsia. To augment his income, he started both learning and teaching Greek. One of his students, William Blount, invited him to England to become a student of Greek at Oxford. There he was introduced to Richard Charnock, the prior of one of the colleges, who in turn brought him to meet Dr John Colet, who was lecturing on the book of Romans at the university. One day Colet took Erasmus for a meal at the home of the Lord Mayor of London and at the table he sparred with a nineteen-year-old boy who sat opposite him, whose name was Thomas More. They were to become lifelong friends. More took Erasmus to the royal nursery to meet the nine-year-old Henry, who was to be the future King Henry VIII. On every occasion, Erasmus dazzled and amazed his hosts with his sharp mind and keen wit.

One of Erasmus' friends enabled him to accomplish a lifelong dream and travel to Italy. Venice was a thrilling experience. At Rome he had a great and flattering reception, meeting cardinals and strengthening his existing friendship with Pope Julius II. The pope asked him to stay and write papers on the pontiff's military activities, but he declined, considering Rome another tempting cage in which he would end up with his wings clipped. On his way back to England he was awarded a doctorate at the University of Turin.

Erasmus owed much of his popularity to his writings. The early poems of the 1490s gave way to his *Manual of the Christian Soldier*, in which he showed that much of the dogma and ceremony in the church were irrelevant. Writings such as this fed the future reform movement. William Tyndale, who was born the year Erasmus died, had the manuscript translated into English, and then printed and circulated.

When Erasmus returned to England in 1505, he stayed with Sir Thomas More and wrote his famous satire *In Praise of Folly*, in which he portrayed kings, bishops, princes and popes in bondage to Folly. But his greatest work was his edition of the Greek New Testament, which appeared in 1516. For this, Erasmus collected the Greek documents of antiquity for the entire New Testament, and compiled and printed them with a Latin translation, on 672 pages. To assure its acceptance, he dedicated it to Pope Leo X.

This was the first time the New Testament in its original language was made generally available—about 3,300 copies were printed of the first two editions. The only other Greek edition available was confined to about 600 unwieldy and expensive copies. Erasmus' edition formed

Erasmus, from a painting by Hans Holbein.

the basis of vernacular translations of the New Testament for much of Europe: Zwingli and Calvin used it to give their people a Bible, Luther did the same for the German nation, and Tyndale for England. The fourth and fifth editions of 1527 and 1536 were used in the King James version. Erasmus had never intended to create such a conflagration, but then, he should have known better than to play with matches. As he himself admitted, he "laid the egg which Luther hatched."

Review

It might be helpful to see where our trail has led us so far.

We have seen that the New Testament writings were the work of apostles or men who knew the apostles. The young church grew rapidly, turning the world upside down. Persecution, far from destroying the church, fanned the fire of faith into a blaze. Though the church was often bitterly split by controversies and heresies, out of these inner turmoils emerged the creeds.

With Constantine there came new dangers. As we shall see in more detail in the next section, the church became materialistic, secular, power-seeking, and immoral. Ritual increased. Preacher gave way to priest, the Lord's table to the altar, the apostle to the pope. Excommunication turned into execution. The Latin Bible was known only to priest and monk, and even then was little studied. Without the Bible, apostasy went unchecked while ordinary people fed on superstition and fear.

91

In the middle of the medieval night, scholasticism opened up an opportunity for debate. In the fourteenth century the voice of reform was heard in the West. Since John Wycliffe's benefactor was the king's brother, every attempt to silence his voice was frustrated.

As humanist learning spread from Constantinople, scholars began to study Erasmus' Greek New Testament. With the invention of printing new and subversive ideas spread rapidly throughout Europe. The door was open at last for the Reformation, and for the collapse of the wall which had divided the people from the indestructible book.

4. The Reformation Reaches England

Overview

This section might well be sub-titled "The earthquake and its after-shocks." It is impossible to exaggerate the impact of the Reformation on Europe. It purged a defiled church, transformed moral attitudes, re-ordered human priorities and placed a book, the "Indestructible Book," at the center of an arena of conflict. But what brought about this continental upheaval?

Europe did not fall in domino effect to the Reformation. Martin Luther did not make Switzerland, France, the Netherlands, Scotland and England reject the rule of Rome. Though there were links between them, these were still independent movements. The responses of reformers in Germany may have been similar to those in Switzerland, but one did not cause the other. They were spontaneous reactions to the same cause: a degraded, immoral and bankrupt church.

Moral conditions

From St Bernard at the beginning of the twelfth century to Bishop Fox, who founded Corpus Christi College, Oxford, in 1516, every generation heard the voices of leading churchmen calling for reform. From 1215 to 1512, there were nine great ecumenical councils, each attempting to deal with the need for church reform. When the Council of Trent was held in 1545, it testified to the impotence of previous councils and witnessed to the increasing immorality of the church. Of the 281 parishes of the diocese of Hereford in 1397, fifty-two were known to the bishop to have priests living with a concubine. In 1450, the Bishop of St Asaph was making a sizable income from selling licenses for concubinage to his priests. This immorality was at the root of the sores which plagued the church, and the discontent which resulted.

Doctrine

Reacting to a church which could countenance such immorality, some people sought to reform the doctrine. An anti-priestly movement began in the twelfth century leading, as we have seen, to the Waldenses, based on the authority of the Bible. The Waldenses, who considered themselves orthodox Catholics, denied any separation between clergy and laity. Though the strongest measures were taken to repress them, in 1200 the heretics in southern France are believed to have outnumbered the Catholics and the ruthless inquisition carried out by Innocent III could not exterminate the cult.

Politics

In 1054 the Christian church divided when the pope in Rome and the patriarch, the head of the church in Constantinople, disagreed about the leadership of the church. Even within the West, the medieval ideal of "one empire and one church" was sorely tested by anti-priestly groups but the western church maintained its power with an iron grip. People were either born into the church or baptized at an early age and any attempt to leave was a crime considered worthy of being burnt to death. The church organization was supported by mandatory tithes and taxes, and for most of the Middle Ages the authority of the pope overrode the secular power of the state. Pope Gregory VII (1028–1085) spelt this out when he asserted that the power to "bind and loose" made every earthly sovereign subservient to the pope.

The situation changed in 1309, when the papacy moved to Avignon, remaining there until 1377. At that time France was the most powerful nation in the West, and the popes found themselves subservient to the French monarchy. Later popes played Italian politics while European princes manipulated them to gain power. These conditions created antagonisms between church and state.

Economics

Clerical possessions were enormous. It is estimated that one fifth to one third of all landed property belonged to the church. Moreover, the church claimed that its property was exempt from state taxation, and this was a source of constant friction. Pope John XXII did not ease the situation when, in the early part of the fourteenth century, he claimed that the pope could appoint whoever he wanted to any church appointments. As we have seen, this led to a systematic trade in benefices at the courts of Rome and exacerbated disagreements between France and England. When the pope needed more money, he sold indulgences. Absolute power had corrupted absolutely.

It would be wrong to say that any of these issues became the single cause of a reformer's action. They gave force to criticism, but the cause of discontent came from the pages of the Bible. It was Martin Luther's

The German Reformer Martin Luther.

teaching on Romans, and his conviction that we are justified by faith, that caused his split with Rome. While Zwingli was disturbed by the insistence on celibacy, and papal disregard of human life, it was his study of Matthew's Gospel and the book of Acts that opened his eyes to his serious disagreements with Rome. Similarly, Calvin was inspired and driven by the teaching of the Bible. In the Netherlands, it was a vernacular transaction of the Old Testament in 1477, and a complete translation based on Luther's German in 1526, that sowed the seeds for conformity to Reformation principles. The Reformation in Sweden dates back to a Lutheran preacher brought to the country by King Christian II of Denmark. In every single instance, it was the liberating truth of the Bible, preached in church pulpits and passed on by Christians, that snapped chains and challenged traditions.

Distant thunder

As the sound of distant thunder announces an approaching storm, so the groans of spiritual discontent in Germany forecast a cataclysmic religious revolution. Martin Luther was born in the village of Eisleben on November 10, 1483. At seven years of age he was sent to a Latin school,

Philip Melanchthon, Luther's fellow reformer.

and graduated in Latin grammar and syntax. At fourteen he was sent to Magdeburg where his teachers were members of the Brotherhood of the Common Life. Four years later, in 1501, he entered the University of Erfurt where, after four years, he earned his B.A. degree, and, after another two years, his M.A. at the age of twenty-two.

By faith alone

One day, during a violent storm, Luther was sheltering under a tree in a forest, when the tree was struck by lightning. His close escape from death startled Luther into spiritual awareness. In July 1505, when he was still twenty-two, he entered the Augustinian monastery at Erfurt, and a year later he took his monastic vows of obedience, poverty and chastity. In 1511 he was transferred to the monastery at Wittenberg where, the next year, he was awarded the degree of Doctor of Theology and became a professor of biblical literature.

In 1517 John Tetzel was making a public nuisance of himself in Wittenberg by selling papal indulgences in order to raise money for the rebuilding of St. Peter's Church in Rome. Indulgences were written promises guaranteeing reduced time in purgatory in return for sums of money, in other words, they were a form of penance by price. Luther strongly resented the practice and publicly disputed with its advocates. At the same time, he was lecturing on the book of Romans. When he came to Paul's words in Romans 1:17: "The just shall live by faith," Luther suddenly understood Paul's doctrine of imputed righteousness and his entire theological framework was shattered. He now saw that a man "in Christ" may have the righteousness of God transferred to his credit "through faith"—and that understanding brought about his great conversion experience.

Ninety-Five Theses

All these factors combined to make Luther write his *Ninety-Five Theses*, criticising the sale of indulgences and many other ecclesiastical abuses, and nail them to the Castle church door in Wittenberg in 1517. This act brought him past the point of no return in his opposition to the Roman Catholic Church, and opened the floodgates to the reform movement in Germany.

In 1518 an order was issued for Luther's arrest, but it was not carried out. In June 1520 Pope Leo X issued a Bull requiring Luther to recant under threat of excommunication.

Diet of Worms

In April 1521 Luther was called before the Diet, or Assembly, of Worms, where he was accused of forty-one errors in doctrine and given sixty days to recant. It is here that Martin Luther is said to have made his immortal statement: "Here I stand. I can do no other . . . my conscience is captive to the Word of God."

On December 10, 1521, Luther publicly burned the papal Bull, and in the fall of the same year he took up his pen again, wielding it against his enemies with all the deadly power of a sword. First he wrote *An Address to the German Nobility*, in which he called for a free council to implement reforms, and informed Christian magistrates that it was their responsibility to care for the church. Two months later, in *The Babylonian Captivity of the Church*, he took issue with the theology of the seven sacraments, denying all but baptism and the Lord's Table. One month later, he wrote his treatise *On the Freedom of the Christian*.

It was obvious that Luther needed the support of the public, sacred and secular, and these writings accomplished that intended goal. Several other publications were still to come, including his greatest theological treatise, *The Bondage of the Will*, written in 1525 in answer to a slander on his theology by the great Erasmus.

The year 1525, when he was forty-two, proved to be a most important year in Luther's life. It was the year when the peasants in Germany rebelled, claiming the support of the gospel in their demand for greater rights. Luther was furious at what he felt was a betrayal of the gospel message. Fearful of anarchy, and afraid that the reform movement would be brought into disrepute if it were linked with the Peasants' Revolt, he wrote an inflammatory condemnation of the revolt entitled *Against the Robbing and Murdering Hordes*. By sharp contrast, 1525 was also the year when he married Katharine von Bora. They had a very happy marriage with three sons and three daughters.

Emperor Charles V (1500–1558).

The Diet of Augsburg

In 1530 the Emperor Charles V called for a meeting at Augsburg at which leaders of the evangelicals could outline their faith. Luther, who was an outlaw, could not attend, and was represented by Philip Melanchthon. After consultation with Luther, Melanchthon drew up a confession of faith which, though it was rejected by the Diet, stands to this day as the digest of Lutheranism.

A Bible for the people

While a rebel attempts to change the past, a reformer intends to change the future, and every religious reformer knew that he could not affect future generations unless he provided them with a vernacular Bible. Therefore the most important years for Luther's pen were those leading up to September 1522, when his German New Testament came off the printing presses.

On May 4, 1521, when he was returning from the Diet of Worms, he was captured in Thuringian forest by a band of thugs and taken as a hostage to Wartburg Castle. It was then that he found out that his captors were friends, working under the orders of Frederick, the Elector of Saxony, his secular protector. Luther's identity was concealed even from those who lived in the castle, and he was known only as "Knight George." While he was there, he prepared manuscripts for the German New Testament, working from the second (1519) edition of Erasmus' New Testament. In Luther's arrangement, Hebrews, James, Jude and Revelation were placed at the end of the publication, as non-canonical.

After the New Testament, Luther started on his translation of the Hebrew Old Testament, finishing it ten years later. Within the first fourteen years of its completion, Luther's Bible, or portions of it, went through 377 editions. Thus he not only taught Europe how to protest against the wrongs of popes and emperors but he made that protest permanent by providing Germany with a copy of the Bible in the language of the people.

Luther had many influential supporters, and this fact, coupled with his formidable ability in theological debate, enabled him to escape torture and death at the hands of state or church. He died of natural causes in the village of Eisleben on February 18, 1546: he came into this world at one end of this little German village, and took his exodus at the opposite end.

Zwingli of Zurich

Switzerland has two languages; the northern part of Switzerland is German-speaking, while the southern part is French-speaking. The dominating city in the German-speaking section is the old medieval city of Zurich, and this city was the headquarters of Ulrich Zwingli, the pioneering reformer of Switzerland, sometimes called "the third man of the Reformation." Born on January 1, 1484, Zwingli was fifty-two days younger than Martin Luther, and he died five years before the other great reformer, John Calvin, started his ministry in Switzerland.

Though his family came from peasant stock, Zwingli's uncle was parish priest at Wildhaus and his father was mayor of Wildhaus. Ulrich received his education in good schools at Wesen, then Basle and finally at Bern. When he was sixteen he left to study philosophy at the University of Vienna, but he returned and graduated from the University of Basle. Then he taught classics in St Martin's church school in Basle.

At twenty-two, he was ordained a priest by the Bishop of Constance, and spent the next ten years as the parish priest at Glarus. It was there that he started his study of Greek and Hebrew, and came under the influence of two outstanding humanists. The first taught him to criticize the doctrines of the Catholic Church; the second, the famous Erasmus, awoke in him a phenomenal interest in the Greek New Testament. By the time of his call to be priest at the Great Minster in Zurich, in 1518, he had been converted to Christ and was already preaching the gospel.

Shortly after Zwingli's arrival in Zurich, a plague swept the city, and his heroic ministry to the people during this time endeared him to them.

Ulrich Zwingli, the reformer of Zurich, who was killed in battle.

The plague that took the lives of a third of the city's population infected Zwingli, and his close brush with death left him more deeply committed to the cause of the gospel.

Reform

On January 1, 1519, Zwingli began a series of discourses on Matthew's Gospel, followed by another from the book of Acts, and then a final series from Paul's letters. These expositions sowed the seeds of reformation, and gave him the courage to go on to preach against fasting, saint worship, and the celibacy of the priests. Between 1522 and 1526 he introduced many reforms, including government by synod, banning of

Luther and Zwingli debate at Marburg; they could not agree on the theology of the Lord's Supper.

indulgences, removal of images, study groups for the clergy and Bible translation. All this infuriated the Church of Rome, and Pope Adrian VI encouraged the citizens of Zurich to turn against Zwingli.

Zwingli was appalled by the senseless destruction of human life in the wars instigated by popes and fought by mercenary soldiers. Within his parish he was very disturbed by the suffering brought upon bereaved families. He saw deaths leaving widowed families within his parish. He had made three visits to Italy as an army chaplain and this opened his eyes to the worldly nature of papal rule.

The cleavage between Zurich and Rome was made worse when Zwingli requested the bishop to licence his marriage to Anna Reinhart. Anna was the widow of a soldier who was killed in 1517, and had been left with three children. When the bishop denied the request, they were secretly married in 1522, but did not make it public knowledge until 1524. They had four more children.

Public debates

When the Roman authorities tried to separate Zwingli from the citizens of Zurich, he requested the postponement of a decision until the matter

had been debated in public. The first disputation, in 1523, was attended by the mayor and the city council. At its conclusion, they decreed that Zwingli should continue preaching the gospel. At the second disputation, held from October 26 to 28 in the same year, he was opposed by Catholic representatives from other Swiss cantons, who were supported by the pope. Again he addressed the city council, together with another 900 citizens who were able to crowd into the Minster. He called his address *The Shepherd who is the True Pastor* and he spoke on "revelation," "reconciliation," and "revolution." He emerged undefeated, the "Hercules of Zurich."

Luther and Zwingli

Philip of Hesse wanted to consolidate the German reform movements, and for this it was necessary to have a conciliatory meeting between the two titanic personalities, Luther and Zwingli. A meeting was arranged at Marburg for three days in October 1529. In the *Articles of Marburg* there were fourteen doctrines on which the two men agreed, but the famous fifteenth, dealing with the Lord's Supper, proved to be the stumbling block. Zwingli could not accept Luther's doctrine of consubstantiation, that is, the view that Christ is literally present in the bread and wine, even though the bread and wine remained unchanged. Zwingli believed that since Christ's body had ascended into heaven it could not be present in the bread of the Lord's Supper. Zwingli represented the position later adopted by other mainline bodies of Protestantism, and he separated from Lutheranism on this one issue.

The Bible

Probably the most significant result of the public debate was the establishment of the Bible as the sole and final authority for all disputes. This resulted in the publication, in 1529, of a Bible translation made by a collegium of scholars under the leadership of Zwingli and his assistant Bullinger. Known as the Zurich Bible, it was a translation from the Hebrew and Greek into the Swiss-German language. This Bible came five years before Luther completed his Bible for the Germans.

Sadly, in October 1531, Zwingli lost his life on a battlefield during the Second Kappel War. One of the enemy soldiers found him dying and asked him if he needed a priest. He gave no response. He was asked the second time, and again said nothing but folded his hands in prayer with his eyes wide open. An exasperated captain drew his sword and thrust it into the reformer.

Discovering that it was Zwingli, a crowd of wild young men gathered and suggested cutting his body into five parts, and sending a section to each of the five cantons. They set up a court of injustice which decided that his body should be quartered and burned. Pigs had been slaughtered the previous night, and someone threw the entrails of the pigs into the same fire. To show his contempt for Zwingli, the executioner turned the embers over, so that the pigs' offal was mixed with Zwingli's ashes.

The giant of Geneva

The Reformation Monument of Geneva was started in 1909, but not completed until 1917. It is composed of ten statues, the four in the center being of four reformers. Why are neither Luther nor Zwingli in this center grouping? It is because it was Presbyterianism and not Lutheranism that was born in Geneva. John Calvin, the pioneer of the system of governing churches by councils of ministers, or presbyteries, is one of the four. On his immediate right is Guillaume Farel, a man twenty years his senior, who preceded him to Geneva by a year, and was instrumental in bringing reformed theology to Geneva. He worked with Calvin in Geneva from 1536 until they were both expelled in 1538.

On the immediate left is Theodore Beza, ten years younger than Calvin and a theologian who in some respects out-Calvined Calvin. He was Calvin's representative for the Reformed movement in France. He wrote a biography of Calvin, and became Calvin's Elisha, taking over as head of the government of Geneva after Calvin's death. On the far left is Scotland's famous John Knox, who claimed to represent Calvin in the Reformation of Scotland.

J.I. Packer described Calvin as "a sallow, sharp-featured, black-haired, slightly-built Frenchman, with big brown eyes that sparkled or glared according to mood. . . . As he aged and his health ebbed he grew bent, gaunt, and emaciated."

Calvin was born at Noyon, France, on July 10, 1509. In 1521, his father sent him to prepare for the priesthood at the University of Paris. This was the same institution that had previously trained Erasmus, and the following year would receive Ignatius Loyola, the founder of the Society of Jesus, known as the Jesuits, which was to be the most successful Roman Catholic counterpart to the Protestant Reformation.

John Calvin, the reformer of Geneva and founder of the Reformed tradition.

After Calvin received his B.A. and M.A. degrees, his father sent him to the University of Orleans, where he obtained another B.A., this time in law. It was during his latter student days that he was converted to Christ and became a supporter of the Protestant Reformation. Upon returning to Noyon he was thrown in prison as a heretic, but mysteriously managed to escape. He eventually arrived back in Paris, but his robust Protestant witness caused a surge of persecution. The city dedicated January 29, 1535 to the solemn event of "purging," six Protestants by torturing them and burning them to death. When it seemed that an official persecution of Protestants would continue throughout France, Calvin fled to Basle and settled there. In March 1536, when he was only twenty-seven, his book, *Institutes of the Christian Religion*, came off the presses. Deciding that it was impossible for him to labor for the gospel in France, he opted to work in Germany, but on his way he was forced to make a detour because of a local war, and passed through Geneva. Guillaume Farel prevailed on him to stay there and they enjoyed two years of joint ministry.

The banishment of Farel and Calvin from Geneva on May 26, 1538 was brought about by several factors. Calvin and Farel had set up a theocracy in the city, declaring that the civic administrators were servants of the church. A catechism was prepared and made binding on all citizens, requiring public acceptance or banishment. Opponents found encouragement from the people of Bern. Opposition grew, and the two reformers were obliged to flee for their safety.

The new city government was weak, and Calvin's supporters treated it with contempt. The Roman Catholic bishop failed in his attempt to take control and Calvin was urged to return and reestablish civil and ecclesiastical order. He came back on September 13, 1541, to a tumultuous ovation, reinstated his theocracy and ruled with an iron fist.

Calvin prepared the "Genevan Catechism" and forced compliance with its doctrine, introducing a system of paid informers to prevent secret transgressions. Between the years 1542 and 1546, some seventy-six people were banished and fifty-eight executions took place including thirty-four women who were burned on suspicion of spreading the plague by magical means. In 1553, Michael Servetus was burned for his heretical views on the Trinity.

From 1549 Geneva became a haven for 6,000 Protestant refugees from England, Scotland and France. John Knox called Geneva "the most perfect school of Christ since the apostles."

Despite any weaknesses he may have had, the Christian world owes a debt of gratitude to this great Reformer. His *Institutes*, revised and enlarged to three times their original size, were a unique theological handbook, the first book of biblical systematic theology of such length. The other Reformers wrote, and argued doctrine, but not to the depth characteristic of Calvin. Second, he built a university. It became the only

St. Giles Cathedral, Edinburgh;
from the pulpit John Knox
preached his fiery sermons.

school for the training of Reformed ministers, and made Geneva the capital city of the Reformed movement. Finally, he assisted in the translation of the Bible known as the Geneva Bible of 1560.

On February 16, 1564, Calvin preached his last sermon; on April 20, he made his will; on May 2, he wrote his last letter, to his friend Farel; on May 27, in the arms of a faithful friend, he slipped out into eternity, and the next day they buried him in a grave we cannot find today.

The timing of Calvin's ministry was providentially appropriate. If Luther started the first Reformation, Calvin fathered a second. If it had not been for the sanctuary and training offered to exiles who fled to Geneva, the English Reformation might have perished before the end of the sixteenth century. His influence has lasted through the centuries: unashamed to be identified with this reformer were great poets such as John Milton, great reformers such as William Wilberforce, great missionaries such as William Carey and great preachers such as George Whitefield and Charles Haddon Spurgeon.

Give me Scotland

John Knox was a small man with a sturdy body; he had a powerful face, with dark blue eyes under bushy eyebrows, high cheek bones, and a long black beard which later turned gray. He was born about 1514. His father, William Knox, was a prosperous peasant and he sent him to university where he studied under John Major. He was ordained a priest, and served, as his signature testifies in 1543, "as a minister of the sacred altar" under the Archbishop of St Andrews.

Some time within the next three years he came under the influence of George Wishart, the reformer. When Wishart was arrested for heresy in December 1546, Knox was among those trying to defend him. But Wishart was imprisoned at Edinburgh Castle, and publicly burned to death at St Andrews the following month. It was a time of unrest in Scotland, which was governed by a council and the French-born queen mother during the infancy of Mary Queen of Scots. Knox traveled from place to place to escape persecution, but when the people of St Andrews rebelled, killed the archbishop and took possession of his castle, Knox returned to become a preacher among them. In the summer of 1547 the French captured the castle, and Knox spent the next nineteen months as a slave on the galleys.

He gained his freedom through the intervention of the Protestant King Edward VI of England, and became a licenced preacher in England. He was appointed as a royal chaplain in 1552, but when Edward died and was succeeded by the Roman Catholic Mary, Knox fled to the continent. He first tried to settle in Frankfurt, but the English congregation was divided and Knox was expelled. He then went to Geneva where he worked on the translation of the Geneva Bible. In 1555 he brought his wife and mother from England and spent the next few years in peace, absorbing the teaching of John Calvin.

In August 1555, on the promise of a permit to preach privately for six months, Knox returned to southern Scotland. He found his native country ruled by the queen mother (the widow of James V of Scotland), while her daughter, Mary Queen of Scots, was being tutored in the courts of France. He received an enthusiastic welcome and, following his advice, people stopped attending mass. As a result of his teaching, the authorities condemned him and burned his effigy.

When he returned to the continent, he left behind *A Letter of Wholesome Counsel*, addressed to the heads of Scottish families, reminding them that they were "bishops and kings" in their own homes. This *Letter* sowed the seeds of the future Reformation in Scotland. In 1558 he addressed another publication, *Appellation*, to the nobles, in which he argued against the death sentence which had been pronounced on him. The following year Knox went to the midlands of Scotland to arouse support. So strongly did he inveigh against the friars that the people sacked the friaries in Perth.

The queen mother, held a prisoner in Edinburgh Castle by the Scottish Protestants, was appealing to the French to come to her rescue. Knox attempted to counter this through an alliance with Elizabeth in England, whose position was threatened by the French. Unfortunately, Knox had just published *The Monstrous Regiment of Women*, bemoaning the sad state of government in Scotland, ruled by women. Elizabeth

Mary Stuart, Mary Queen of Scots.

took offense and it delayed the formation of an alliance. The French landed and drove the government forces out of Edinburgh during the night. Utterly despondent, they retreated to Stirling, but Knox aroused their courage again by a sermon, and English troops arrived in time to rescue them, forcing the French to retreat from Scotland.

This was the year that Knox lost his first wife, who died before she could witness the victory over the French. Knox persuaded a seventeen-year-old girl to become his second wife, and they enjoyed a happy marriage. The new Scottish legislative body, the Estates, met for the first time in August 1560, and requested a Protestant Confession of Faith. Knox and others formulated this, and it stood as the only Scottish creed for the next two centuries. It became the basis of three Acts: the first abolished the authority of the pope in Scotland, the second rescinded all old statutes with Catholic tenets, and the third outlawed any celebration of the Mass, making it punishable by death. At this point the Reformation was complete in Scotland.

When the queen mother died in Edinburgh Castle in 1561, Mary Queen of Scots returned to rule Scotland, posing a challenge to Knox's leadership. As a devout Catholic, she observed the Mass privately in her palace, and public opinion restrained Knox from doing anything about it. Four interviews took place between Mary and Knox, but queen and preacher were both resolute and unbending, using their wits to make thrusts against each other. When Mary married the Catholic Henry Darnley, the Protestant lords went into exile, fearing that the Reformation in Scotland was over, but Knox continued preaching at St Giles in Edinburgh. When Darnley agreed to attend a service at St Giles church, Knox preached about Ahab and Jezebel, inveighing against a government of "babes and women." Mary was furious and persuaded a number of the lords to issue an edict forbidding Knox to preach while she was resident in Edinburgh. In 1566 Knox was forced into hiding, and he remained silent until, in 1567, the Queen was imprisoned in the castle at Lochleven on suspicion of having had Darnley murdered. Knox then returned to Edinburgh and reestablished the Reformation. Mary abdicated and her child James VI of Scotland was crowned as an infant king.

John Knox (c1514–72), Scots reformer.

In 1570, Knox had a stroke and retired to St Andrews where he wrote his will and published his last book. He wrote in that book: "For as the world is weary of me, so am I of it." In the autumn of 1572 he returned to Edinburgh, living with his wife and their three daughters in a quaint and picturesque house, across from St Giles. He died on November 24, 1572.

Till death us do part

To take part in the Reformation in England was to take part in a great adventure of spirit and mind. The fifteenth century was an age of thrills and revolution. It was a new age in geography. A forty-one-year-old

King Henry VIII.

Italian adventurer, Columbus, had set out from Spain in 1492 and rediscovered America. In 1497, Vasco da Gama sailed out from Portugal and established a sea route to India. Weather-beaten ships, with tattered sails, were tying up to docks in different ports around the world. Sunburnt sailors were bringing back to Europe strange stories of remote lands and new customs.

It was also a new age in astronomy. In 1513 Nicolaus Copernicus, a Polish astronomer, began to remap the heavens. His discoveries overturned all previous ideas about the movements of the earth and planets.

It was also an age of reform in other sciences. As we have seen, in 1453 Constantinople had fallen to Muhammad II and the Greek population fled to the West. They infiltrated all the major centers of Western Europe, bringing with them the language and culture of ancient Greece, awakening interest in the arts and introducing new ideas to architecture, sculpture, painting and music. Leonardo da Vinci, Bernini and Michelangelo became common household names.

Finally, it was a new age in theology. The English Reformation stands in sharp contrast to the reformations of Germany, France, the Low Countries, Switzerland and Scotland, which were inspired by strong, dominating and unbending leaders. No such leader existed in England. Rather, change came about from the interplay of a number of factors including political and social conditions, the barrenness of humanism and a renewed interest in the Bible.

To understand the political climate which fostered the Reformation in England, it is helpful to look at two things.

The first was the marital difficulties faced by Henry VIII. Henry VII was on the throne when his oldest son Arthur died in 1502, six months after his marriage to Catherine of Aragon, daughter of Ferdinand and Isabella of Spain. The marriage was part of a political alliance, and it was the concern of politicians that the alliance should not be broken by Arthur's sudden death. So they arranged for the betrothal of Arthur's younger brother, Henry, to Catherine. Henry was only eighteen years old in 1509, when Henry VII died and the boy became King Henry VIII. Shortly after his coronation Henry and Catherine were married. Catherine was six years older than Henry and, because of difficulties in the interpretation of the Old Testament law concerning marriage by brothers (see Leviticus 20:21), a papal dispensation was required for the marriage. In view of the importance of England and Spain, the pope was quick to offer divine consent.

Catherine and Henry had seven children. Three were stillborn and only a girl, the future "Bloody Mary," survived infancy. Henry had a mistress, who gave birth to a son, and this led Henry to wonder if Catherine's inability to provide him with a male heir was God's judgement on her. He petitioned the pope for an annulment, and a dispensation to marry Anne Boleyn. But the pope, having approved the marriage

on God's behalf, would not now condone its dissolution.

The reformers made full use of Henry's dilemma to wean the English throne away from its dependence on the papal chair at the Vatican. Thomas Cranmer was the first to suggest to the King that the important thing to know was what the Bible taught, and that perhaps Parliament, or the faculty of the universities, were better suited to deliberate such issues than the Vatican. The king seized the opportunity, appealed for their decision, and made Cranmer the next Archbishop of Canterbury.

The second political factor was the Roman Church's misuse of its power in England. In 1506, the first stone was put in place for the building of the new basilica at the Vatican, for which more money was needed. Already the churches in England were draining the country's coffers: it is estimated that the Vatican took five times more money than the crown. This was particularly repugnant in the light of the church's moral bankruptcy. In 1529 Simon Fish published *A Supplication for Beggars*, and addressed it to the king. He reminded the king that these "holy men" were so immoral that it affected "every man's wife . . . daughter . . . and maid." This was not something that was confined to one local region, but was rampant and countrywide. He wrote: "They [the monks] have a hundred thousand idle whores in England."

It is impossible to estimate what success the Reformation might have enjoyed in England if it had not been set against this background.

The Achilles heel

Opposition to the Reformation in England came from two sides, like a pincer movement, in the form of religious opposition from the established church, and philosophic opposition from the new humanist movement in scholarship.

The religious opposition was to be expected, as the two theologies were antagonistic in every respect. Thomas Wolsey, the last Roman Catholic primate of England, epitomized the Church at its worst. The son of a wealthy butcher and inn-keeper in Ipswich, he graduated from Magdalen College, Oxford, in 1490, when he was only fifteen years of age. Nine years later he was ordained a priest. Wolsey had enormous administrative gifts, and proved to be a very clever politician. He quickly rose to power, becoming a chaplain to Henry VII who employed him in diplomatic work. When Henry VII died, Wolsey immediately became almoner to twelve-year-old Henry VIII, and greatly influenced the young king, playing games with him and suggesting that his life should be enjoyed, and that the tedious running of government should be left to others. In 1511 he became a member of the Privy Council, and thereby secured a controlling voice in the government. In 1514 Pope Leo X made him Archbishop of York, the second highest ecclesiastical position in England.

He was a devoted Roman Catholic, dedicated to the advancement of the Church in England. He became recognized as the leader in the crusade to stamp out heretics and introduced a period of terror in which many godly people suffered loss of property and imprisonment, and some were burned to death. He assumed that his reputation, and his circle of influential friends, would obtain for him the papal chair at the death of Leo X, but the effort failed. When Pope Adrian VI died a little over a year later, Wolsey made another effort to get himself selected as the next pope. But letters, pressures and conniving all failed again. Six years later, when the next pope died suddenly while celebrating Mass, Wolsey made a third passionate effort, which also failed. According to

Cardinal Thomas Wolsey, whose death removed a major obstacle to the Reformation in England.

reports, he was driven in his quest more by his passion for power than his thirst for spiritual leadership.

Wolsey's egotism was equal only to that of the king himself. Sustained by the support of both pope and king, he assumed the privileges of royalty. He had servants serve him on their knees, bishops tie his shoe latchets and dukes hold the basin while he washed his hands. He used his awesome power entirely for his own ends. He dressed in silks and scarlet velvet, and lived in opulent splendor at Hampton Court. With its 500 rooms and 44 acres of garden, it exceeded the grandeur of the royal residence of Henry VIII himself. He was also notoriously immoral and it is recorded that he fathered several illegitimate children. Eventually the laity and the clergy turned against him.

While it lasted Wolsey's power was almost without bounds, but his position was always precarious. He walked a tight-rope, balancing the demands of king and pope. Trouble arose when the pope's authority infringed upon the authority held by the king. Ultimately, Wolsey's authority came from the pope. If Wolsey could have persuaded the pope to grant a divorce from Catherine of Aragon, he would not have fallen from power, the reformers would not have gained access to the king, and, humanly speaking, the Reformation in England would not have succeeded.

A divorce from Catherine, followed by marriage to a Protestant, was tantamount to political divorce from Rome. Wolsey could see the handwriting on the wall. He could not change Henry's mind on the divorce, nor on remarriage to Anne Boleyn. He realized that Anne's acceptance was automatically his rejection, and he would inevitably fall from favor. It became obvious that, as one historian worded it, "a thousand Wolseys" were not worth "one Anne Boleyn."

When the Cardinal saw that he had over-stepped his bounds, he sought and obtained permission from the king to withdraw to York. This was the first time he had been there despite becoming its archbishop sixteen years earlier. At Easter 1530 he set out for York in his customary splendor, with a retinue of 160 people. All he wanted now was to be left alone, but it was too late; he had offended and harmed too many people, common and high. The Lords listed forty-four grievances against him, and presented them to the king, who sent them to the Commons, where the charge of treason was made against him. In 1530 King Henry sent Sir William Kingston, then constable of the Tower of London, with an escort of twenty-four guards, to bring him to London for trial. Wolsey was terrified. He paced his bedroom, talked to himself and sat down and cried like a baby.

On the way down from Yorkshire, they stopped at Leicester Abbey for the night, and there terror, anguish and torment seized the Cardinal. He said to Kingston: "Tell that king that I conjure him in God's name to destroy this new pernicious sect of Lutherans." He added: "If he tolerates heresy, God will take away his power." It was with difficulty that he uttered these words. His tongue began to falter and his eyes became fixed. He died as the clock struck eight. The last obstacle placed by Rome in the path of the Reformation was removed.

The quack's potion

The other anti-Reformation force was humanism, which stood in direct opposition to everything which the reformers believed in. Humanism was based on the tenet of man's innate goodness, while the reformers declared that man was utterly depraved. Humanism focused on human effort; the reformers relied on God's grace. Humanism suggested that redemption could be found in college; the reformers believed it could only be found at Calvary. The two leading humanists in England were John Colet and Sir Thomas More, and both were helped by Erasmus of Rotterdam.

John Colet

Colet was the son of Sir Henry Colet, twice the Lord Mayor of London. John studied at Oxford, where in 1490 he earned his M.A. degree. He left for Paris three years later, then went to Italy to study canon and civil law as well as Greek, returning in 1496. During his travels he met several

Dean Colet, humanist Bible scholar.

people who greatly influenced him, including Savonarola, a Dominican friar and preacher who denounced Italian corruption and sensuality. When he returned to England, he was ordained and began expounding the letters of St Paul at Oxford University. He did not approach his subject in the old scholastic manner, but he explained the content of the letters, stressing the personality of the apostle and the times in which Paul lived. This started a new trend in biblical exegesis which greatly influenced other scholars. In 1504 he became the Dean of St Paul's Cathedral and four years later, when his father died, and he inherited his wealth, he restructured the school at St Paul's so that it provided a Christian education including Greek and Latin for the 153 students who were being trained there. In 1514, in the company of Erasmus, he made a pilgrimage to Canterbury, and the following year he preached at the installation of Wolsey as Cardinal.

While he was a staunch Catholic, he was also a humanist. He was a fat man, who loved to eat well, and was a generous host, who gave elegant and sumptuous dinner parties. The leading humanists of the day met around his table. His influence was of cardinal importance to that movement, and his house was deemed to be the birthplace and center of humanism in England. He died in 1519 in Sheen, Surrey.

Sir Thomas More

The second most powerful voice for humanism in England was that of Sir Thomas More, who was born in London on February 7, 1478. His father wished him to pursue a legal career and this brought him to Oxford, where he fell under the influence of John Colet and embraced humanism.

Much could be said in praise of Sir Thomas: he represented the best of Roman Catholicism. He was a sincere and devout man who avoided the debauchery of the times. He submitted to fasts and vigils, and scourged himself every Friday. He would sleep on the bare ground, using a log for a pillow, and limit himself to five hours' sleep a night. He wore a shirt of hair-cloth and mortified his body with small chains next to his skin. When he had almost committed himself to taking priest's orders, a meeting with Jane Colt changed his resolve, and they were married in 1505.

The great Erasmus first met him in the home of the Lord Mayor of London. More was only nineteen at the time, but could converse in Latin, Greek, French or English. While still studying law, he gave public lectures on Augustine's *City of God*. He was opposed to the reformers on religious and philosophical grounds, and also opposed the king's divorce, at great personal cost.

He slowly climbed the ladder of success. The lawyer became a judge, and in 1510 the judge became under-sheriff of London. He became the Chancellor of the Duchy of Lancaster, and every effort was made to

Sir Thomas More, humanist scholar and enemy of the Reformation.

attach him to the royal court. Eventually, in 1529, when a replacement was needed for Wolsey, Thomas More was given the position of Chancellor of England, the first layman ever to hold that office. The Lord Chancellor is the first officer of state in England, ranking next in precedence to members of the royal family and the Archbishop of Canterbury. He is also president of the House of Lords. Unlike Wolsey, More carried out his office with dignity and moral restraint.

It is a paradox that those who fought for "free thinking" should have behaved with intolerance towards those whose philosophy differed from theirs. In 1531, for example, James Bainham, a distinguished lawyer, met with some believers to study the Bible at a warehouse in Bow Lane. He was arrested and brought to More's home in Chelsea, where he was interrogated by both More and Stokesley, the Bishop of London. When he did not answer their questions according to their liking, he was tied to the "truth tree" in the Chancellor's garden and severely whipped.

More's story ends like Wolsey's. When Parliament passed the act proclaiming the king to be "the sole and supreme head on earth of the Church of England," More refused to comply. He was arrested and put in the Tower, where he spent fifteen months, visited daily by his daughter, who pleaded with him to recant. The authorities hoped that under her constant pressure his courage would fade and he would recant. But he held to his principles. On July 1, 1535, he was placed on trial for high treason. Five days later was executed just outside the Tower, and his head was affixed to London Bridge.

So the two brilliant voices for humanistic philosophy were silent and the reformers kept their vigilant watch on England.

A London statue of Sir Thomas More.

Nineteen days in May

Before going on to see how the first English Bible came to be written, we pause to look at some of the people who, by their prayers and love of God's Word, helped it on its way. Among those who read, believed and distributed the English Bible throughout the kingdom was Anne Boleyn. In many respects she was to the court of Henry VIII what Esther had been to the Persian court of the fifth century BC.

Born the daughter of Sir Thomas Boleyn, Anne spent her childhood days at Hever Castle in Kent. When she was about twelve, she lived for three years in the French royal household, returning in 1522 to become part of the English court. She had an oval face, bright eyes and black hair. Her beauty, her polished manners and graceful deportment soon brought her to the attention of the king. She had a sweet singing voice and danced with dignity. When Henry was despondent, her songs and laughter attracted him like a magnet. He wrote to her frequently, mostly in French, and spoke of "the great love I have for you". But he was married, and she had no intention of becoming his mistress. This affection, which became an unfulfilled passion, deepened Henry's determination to have her for himself. With his divorce from Catherine in sight, Henry proposed marriage, but Anne declined his offer. The king then solicited help from her father, and at last she yielded. "If the king becomes free," she said, "I shall be willing to marry him."

By December 1528, the king had installed Anne in the palace at Greenwich, giving her Catherine's rooms next to his own while Catherine was sent to Hampton Court. In a secret ceremony on or about January 25, 1533, the couple celebrated their wedding. On May 23 Archbishop Cranmer wrote a letter of confirmation, declaring Henry's marriage to Catherine to be null and void. (The offspring of that union, the future Queen Elizabeth, was born eight months later, on September 7.) It was not until May 28 that, with great public celebration, Anne was proclaimed Queen of England. The couple stayed at the Tower during these festivities.

ANNA BOLINA VXOR- ⋯ HENRI- OCTA

Anne was a sweet, graceful lady who openly supported the reform movement. She attempted to influence secretary Cromwell to overlook the crimes of a group of people who were caught smuggling Tyndale's New Testaments into England. Her own specially bound copy is preserved in the British Library. She was a generous patron of students both at Oxford and Cambridge and abroad, and appointed a noted reformer, Matthew Parker, to become chaplain to her daughter Elizabeth. Finally, Anne frequently mediated with the king to promote reformers, and seven of the ten bishops appointed between 1532 and her death were reformers whom she had supported.

But the love that had once burned in the king's heart turned cold in less than three years. The king's fancies veered towards Jane Seymour, and this so troubled Anne that she gave premature birth to a dead son. One day, in January 1536, she walked into a room unexpectedly and found her husband in a compromising position with Jane Seymour. From then on she expected something to happen to her, but what would it be, and when?

Anne Boleyn, to marry whom Henry VIII severed with the Roman Catholic Church.

On May 1, 1536, a magnificent festival was prepared at Greenwich. The spectators were in a gala spirit as they waited for the jousting to begin. When the queen accidentally dropped her handkerchief, Henry Norris, one of the chief jousters, picked it up and wiped his face. At once, the king left his position and returned to London, while the queen, greatly distressed, followed in an effort to find out what the problem was. The next day Kingston, the lieutenant of the Tower, arrived at her apartments. He escorted her by barge up the Thames to the Tower, and imprisoned in the very suite of rooms she had occupied with the king during her coronation ceremonies.

When archbishop Cranmer heard of her arrest, he was stunned and did not accept any charges brought against her. Three gentlemen, including the young man who had picked up her handkerchief, and a musician, were arrested and interrogated, accused of acts of adultery with the queen. The first two men strongly denied the charges, but when the musician was put on the body rack he quickly agreed to any statements his torturers wished. They were all sentenced to death, including the queen. Cranmer cannot be defended for his duplicity in these events: at the king's command he signed their death sentence.

At 11 a.m. on May 19, Anne calmly laid her head on a block of wood inside the Tower grounds, at a site still commemorated today. A Frenchman noted for his skills as an executioner performed the act, and a cannon shot was fired from the Tower to inform the king that Anne was dead.

Revenge is sweet

Henry VIII was the husband of six wives, the lover of several concubines and the father of many children, legitimate and illegitimate; but only three children survived infancy, and only one was a boy. The three children were Mary, Elizabeth and Edward; and Edward automatically became the heir to the throne. Archbishop Cranmer baptized him and stood as one of his godfathers. Edward was deeply influenced by the Reformed faith and was Protestant to the core. But his health was poor and his life was short. He was born in October, 1537, ascended the throne when he was nine years old, and departed this life in July, 1553, in the middle of his fifteenth year. The male line was finished, and Henry's daughter Mary, over twenty-one years older than Edward, inherited the throne.

Queen Mary I

In contrast to her brother, Mary had been baptized by Cardinal Wolsey, who became her godfather. On the grounds that her mother, Catherine of Aragon, had not been lawfully married to Henry, she had been treated as a bastard child, and had even been required to act as a lady in waiting to

ANNO DNI

ADI MARI
HE MOST
ING HENRI

DOVGHTER
VERTVOVS PR
THE EIGHT

THE AGE OF

XXVIII YER

Queen Mary I, during whose reign many Protestants were martyred.

her half-sister Elizabeth, the daughter of her mother's successor. She was twenty when her mother died, and was not even allowed to be by her side to bid her farewell. Her days till she became queen were harrowing and tense, with the threat of murder never far away.

When she became queen, she was as committed to the Catholic Church as her brother had been to the Protestant faith. Insisting that it was her right to observe the Mass in her private chapel, she appealed to her cousin, the Emperor Charles V, who threatened war on the issue of her religious freedom.

At the beginning of Mary's reign her throne was threatened by Lady Jane Grey, a sixteen-year-old girl who could speak Greek and Latin fluently, and had some knowledge of Hebrew. Her titled father had brought her to the royal court where she had attracted the attention of Northumberland, the most powerful political figure in England. He arranged her marriage to his fourth son, Lord Dudley, and on Edward's death, Northumberland persuaded a faction of leading Protestant reformers to crown Jane Queen of England. When the young girl heard the news, she fainted, and then strongly protested, but finally succumbed to the pressure exerted upon her.

This display of Protestant political power terrified Mary and she scurried for safety to the county of Norfolk in the east of England. Parliament, however, had already decreed that if Edward should die without a son, the throne legitimately belonged to Mary. Lady Jane Grey was therefore dethroned after nine days, tried for treason and executed at the Tower of London.

Mary unveiled her intentions to marry. Her choice was Philip, the son of the emperor Charles, eleven years her junior. The decision was both politically and personally unfortunate. Parliament tried to persuade Mary against the match, but without success, and at the news of the proposed match rebellions broke out all over the country. One rebel force, led by Wyatt, was at the gates of London before it was quelled. Following the defeat of Wyatt, Mary married Philip and determined to reestablish the Catholic religion in England. Philip's father was at war in Europe, and the son was called to Brussels to head the government of the Low Countries, and, later, of Spain. He returned to London only long enough to involve England in the war, then left for the continent, never to return again.

Persecution

At the beginning of her reign, Mary displayed a gentle disposition and a forgiving spirit; but her attitude changed as her position grew more secure. A dark cloud fell then on the reformers' cause. The decline in the fortunes of Archbishop Cranmer served as a barometer to reveal Mary's changing attitudes. It was he who had crowned Lady Jane Grey and, worse still, had declared the divorce of the Queen's mother to Henry VIII. At first he was placed under house arrest, and then, on September 14, 1553, was sent to the Tower of London where he joined Hugh Latimer and Nicholas Ridley, the Bishop of London. These men had been arrested before Wyatt's rebellion. In March 1554 the three were sent to Oxford for their trial. Latimer and Ridley were executed on October 16, 1555; Thomas Cranmer faced his ordeal in the flames on March 21, 1556.

The first English Protestants to be condemned to death by burning were Bishop John Hooper of Gloucester and John Rogers. Bishop Hooper was outstandingly zealous for the truth, and consequently on January 29, 1555, he was put on trial for heresy. When he refused to recant, the death sentence was pronounced, and John Hooper was turned over to the secular powers.

Nine days before Hooper's execution, John Rogers—condemned at the same trial as Hooper—was burned to death at Smithfield. He was the man who had edited "Matthew's Bible" under the alias of Thomas

Bishop John Hooper of Gloucester, martyred for his faith.

Matthew, eighteen years earlier (see pages 149–51). When he walked from the infamous Newgate prison to the burning site at Smithfield on Monday, February 4, 1555, his wife and children stood among the throng and watched; he was not allowed to speak to them.

The reading of the Bible in the churches, which had been encouraged under Edward VI, was once more discouraged, and a migration of people of the Reformed faith left England for the "free" cities of Europe. However, Mary's reign proved to be short. Her health was delicate both before and after her ascension to the throne, and on November 17, 1558, she died without an heir. She was followed by Elizabeth, and doors which had been closed to the Reformation were opened once more.

The Smithfield Heroes

A memorial should be erected to the men and women who were burned to death in Smithfield. They were all courageous, but some of them revealed uncommon valor. They were not, by and large, taken against their will, but consented to their ordeals. They endured because their convictions, like shafts of steel, would not let them bend even under excruciating pain or terrifying threats. Some of them were weak enough, at moments, to recant; but then found the courage to face their ordeals afresh.

Some were burly men; some were fragile and sensitive women; all were heroes.

In medieval times "Smoothfield," as it was then called, was a large open area. A court clown named Rahere bought the ground from the king and built a church and a hospital on it, dedicating them to St Bartholomew. Every year the St Bartholomew's Fair was held on the property. The week-long festivity included market, jousts, tournaments and

executions. In 1724 Benjamin Franklin was to work in the printing shop housed in the disused church, and John Wesley came to preach there in 1747. "Bart's" hospital continues to this day—the oldest in England.

When people—usually gentlemen—were beheaded, it was normally at Tower Hill; when they were hanged—usually common people—it was at Tyburn; and when they were burned—those guilty of religious crimes—it was at Smithfield. Henry VIII used Smithfield as the

place of execution for religious crimes, but he did not limit himself to burning.

For example, in 1531, thinking it would aid the cause, the Bishop of Rochester's cook tried to poison his master, who was antagonistic to the Reformation. He was found out, and the King had him slowly boiled to death at Smithfield. When Dr Robert Barnes, the Prior of a famous Augustinian monastery in Cambridge, was burned in 1540, two other reformers were burned with him, tied against the same stake. But Henry VIII, not wanting to be considered prejudiced, had three Catholics executed at the same time. They, however, were hanged. Another case is

Four Protestants martyred at Smithfield, London.

is that of John Fisher, the Bishop of Rochester, who was decapitated for refusing to accept the declaration of Parliament that the king was the sovereign head of the Church of England. John Tewkesbury was burned at Smithfield on December 20, 1531. When the flames engulfed him, he gave one last shout—"Christ alone!" Young John Frith, an associate of William Tyndale, was given the opportunity to escape, but declined it for the privilege of publicly witnessing for Christ in his death. When he was tied to the stake and the flames came up around him, he stretched his arms around them, as though they were his friends.

Another hero among the ashes was named John Nicholson, but referred to as Lambert. He was a minister who believed that Christ was present at the communion in the believer's heart and not in the bread and wine. When he was called to account for this error, he appealed to the king and was tried at Westminster Hall on Friday, November 16, 1538, in the king's presence. Four days later he was burned at Smithfield. As he died, he held his burning hands out towards the people and shouted, "None but Christ! None but Christ!"

Anne Askew was the last victim of Henry VIII's reign. She was the second daughter of Sir William Askew, a nobleman from Lincolnshire. When her older sister, who was engaged to a wealthy neighbor, died before the wedding, the father

Two Smithfield martyrs at the stake, 1552.

Three women martyred at Smithfield, 1556.

offered Anne in her place. The marriage was a mismatch. Anne was a devoted disciple of the Reformation principles, and her husband was a devout Catholic. Eventually, he threw her out of his house. She went to London where she was invited to attend prayer and Bible study meetings in the Queen's private apartments. Those leaders with strong Catholic commitment determined to make Anne an example to all the others whom they were afraid to challenge so, at the age of twenty-five, she was thrown into Newgate.

On June 28, 1546, Anne was condemned to be burned at Smithfield. In an attempt to force her recantation, her enemies placed her on the body rack at the prison. She fainted, but remained steadfast, saying, "I'd sooner die than break my faith." When they took her to Smithfield they had to carry her. They tried again to get her to recant, but she replied: "I am not come hither to deny my Lord and Master." It was late evening on July 16, 1546, and the night sky over London was lit up with the flames that released her spirit to meet with the other heroes of Smithfield.

PASSING THE BATON

In 1517, the year Martin Luther nailed his Theses to the church door at Wittenberg, and the year Thomas Bilney bought his illegal copy of the Erasmus New Testament, John Foxe was born in Boston, Lincolnshire. He was destined to become the historian of the Reformation and we are deeply indebted to him for his accounts of many martyrdoms.

His father died when John was young, and his mother then married a very godly man. At Oxford, John earned both his B.A. and his M.A. degrees with credit and in 1539 became a Fellow of Magdalen College. Though originally a devoted follower of the Roman Catholic Church, his studies eventually led him to doubt some issues in its faith and practice. Deeply upset, he would often study all night, and take solitary walks in a grove near the college, meditating on his findings and their implications. He began to attend Mass less frequently and avoid the company of his peers. Too upright to conceal his change of opinions, he resigned his fellowship and in 1545 returned to his home in Boston.

His step-father had no sympathy for his new opinions, and used the anti-heresy laws to rob him of his inheritance and drive him from home. It was in this condition that he met and married Agnes Randall. He earned his living working as a tutor until the accession of Mary to the throne forced him to leave England.

Foxe moved to Strasbourg, bringing with him the Latin manuscript of some notes he had compiled on Christian persecutions from the time of Wycliffe until the year 1500. The work was

John Foxe, chronicler of the Protestant martyrs.

published in Strasbourg in 1554, and constituted the first volume of his *Acts and Monuments*. He then moved to Frankfurt, where he found a group of English refugees, some of whom were Anglicans and others Calvinists. Failing to form a compromise between them, he moved to Basle, and worked as a printer's reader for Johann Herbst. Two years later he published a request to the British nobility to learn toleration. He continued to work on his martyrology, finishing the Latin version in 1559.

Returning to England, Foxe settled in Aldgate where he joined John Day, who had also been a refugee and now owned a printing firm. In 1560 the

Bishop of London, Edmund Grindal, ordained Foxe to the priesthood. It is maintained that he was a prebendary at Salisbury Cathedral, and possibly a rector of Cripplegate; we know that he frequently preached at Paul's Cross, and at other locations. Had he not been committed to puritan principles it is most probable that he would have risen in prominence in the ecclesiastical world.

In 1563, the first English edition of his *Acts and Monuments of these Latter and Perilous Days* came off John Day's presses. The persecutions during the reign of Mary Tudor were still fresh in people's minds, and the publication was an instant success. Its vivid descriptions and

graphic narrative intensified anti-Roman sentiments during Elizabeth's reign. In 1570, a second edition was published with much new material, and the following year Convocation ordered it to be placed in every cathedral church. It became the leading text book for the period of history with which it dealt, serving as a reading guide for private education. Until the publication of Bunyan's *Pilgrim's Progress* a hundred years later it was second only to the Bible in popularity. One historian records: "Foxe was an indefatigable searcher of old registers, and left them as he found them, after he had made his collections and transcriptions out of them, many whereof I have seen and do possess. . . . Many have diligently compared his books with registers and council books, and have always found them faithful."

Foxe died on April 18, 1587, at seventy years of age, and was buried at St Giles, Cripplegate, in London. But for him we would have remained ignorant of the debt of gratitude we owe to that army of martyrs whose courage helped bring about the free circulation of the Bible in English.

5. The First English Bibles

The pioneer

Just as it is sometimes very difficult to find the source of a mighty river, so it is not always easy to find the beginning of a mighty movement. The German Reformation had its Luther; Switzerland its Zwingli and Calvin; and Scotland its thundering voice of Knox. But in the English Reformation there was no one great human voice. The voice was simply the word of God in the indestructible book. But as the movement progressed, individual people had important roles to play. The man who may perhaps be called the initiator in the translation of the Bible into English was a man called Thomas Bilney.

Bilney was born in Norfolk around 1495. In 1517, he was at Trinity Hall in Cambridge, studying canon law, the subject usually taken by aspiring priests such as Bilney. Canon law had its beginning when Roman law and church policy were in disagreement, and major church councils had to be held. Records were kept of the decisions, and by the fifth century these were collected into "canons." Later, the decrees of individual bishops were added, and by AD 1140 they were compiled into Gratian's *Decretum*, which became a major field of study and reference for future priests.

Bilney's religious life was barren. Fasting, vigils and indulgences had left him with little money (forgiveness being expensive), poor health (he was too frail physically for additional penance), and an empty heart, because through it all he found no peace.

Afraid that every generation had its Judas and that he was the one for his generation, he decided he might as well go to hell for good reasons. One night he went out and bought a blackmarket copy of the Erasmus New Testament, which had been published the previous year and, though banned, was part of the religious sub-culture in Cambridge. As he read it, Bilney was thrilled and stunned. When he read Paul's words in 1 Timothy 1:15 they went like an arrow to his heart. On the spot, he trusted in the Christ of those pages and his life turned upside down. Doubt gave way to assurance, hostility was exchanged for peace, and an

Ely Cathedral, Cambridgeshire. Thomas Bilney was licensed to preach by the Bishop of Ely.

effervescent joy dominated his heart. At once he wanted to share his new-found faith with others.

He picked the White Horse Inn for the field in which to sow the seed. Nicknamed "Little Germany" because Luther's writings were often discussed there, the White Horse was a meetingplace for the scholars of Cambridge who gathered to talk about subjects prohibited in the classroom. Bilney brought his New Testament to these discussion tables and the result was cataclysmic.

The news spread through Cambridge and began to attract notable lecturers from the university. These men came to the White Horse out of curiosity, and were converted as they read and discussed Bilney's New Testament. They included Thomas Arthur, a Fellow of St John's College, who became Bilney's traveling companion; and the famous Hugh Latimer, though he was converted in the confessional booth rather than in the pub. George Stafford, an influential young Fellow of Pembroke Hall, also joined their ranks. He was probably the most admired professor of Cambridge, and his conversion shook the entire academic world. Stafford tried to influence Robert Barnes, another Doctor of Divinity, who was the prior of a monastery in Cambridge. What Stafford failed to achieve, Bilney accomplished, and Robert Barnes became a convert.

The stir aroused all England, attracting other men, such as Matthew Parker, the future Archbishop of Canterbury; William Tyndale, the martyr who, as we will go on to see, was the man who gave England its first English printed Bible; and John Frith, an eighteen-year-old student of mathematics, the brains of the Reformation.

Bilney graduated with a Bachelor of Laws degree and was admitted to holy orders in 1519. In 1525 he was licenced to preach by the Bishop of Ely, and started to proclaim the gospel from the pulpit, denouncing

The elaborate gatehouse to King's College, Cambridge, where John Frith was an undergraduate.

the worship of saints and relics. In 1527 he was arrested while preaching in Ipswich, and taken to the Tower of London. At his trial in the chapter house in Westminster, his judges included Cardinal Wolsey, the Archbishop of Canterbury, and several bishops and lawyers. Wolsey had to depart on urgent business, leaving Tunstall, Bishop of London, in charge. They played cat and mouse with Bilney. His friends were allowed to talk to him, and, on the grounds that it would be "for the benefit of the movement," they succeeded in undermining his resolve. On December 7, 1527, he signed his recantation. The following Sunday, with his head shaven and bare, he walked to St Paul's where he heard a sermon denouncing his heresy, and was forced to light a fire under a stack of Tyndale's Bibles. This shattered his soul and left him almost demented. He resolved to get arrested again so that he could make a stand for the truth.

His second trial took place in 1531 at Norwich, where he had ministered. His public burning there was intended to put an end to his influence. The night before his death, he was eating a hearty meal when Matthew Parker and some friends came to visit him. They tried to comfort him before the horrible ordeal of the following day, but Bilney said nothing. When he had finished eating his meal, he slipped down the bench to where they were sitting, put his open Bible on the table beside him, held his index finger over the flame of the candle and burned it to the bone. He looked at his stunned friends and pointed to Isaiah 43:2: "When thou walkest through fire, thou shalt not be burned."

His captors took Bilney from his cell on the morning of August 19, 1531. As they crossed the Bishop's Bridge he ran forward to embrace the stake and thank God for the privilege of having a second opportunity to die for Christ. He was a noble example to his contemporaries. First, he taught the reformers how to live for Christ, and then he taught them how to die for Him.

Thomas Bilney tests the fire with his finger.

The superintendent

Archbishop Thomas Cranmer.

Thomas Cranmer was very different from most heroes of the Reformation; in fact, he was more of a coward than a hero. But his very ability to bend under pressure enabled him to play a vital role among the promoters of the "Indestructible Book."

He was born in Nottinghamshire on July 2, 1489. Recalling his schooldays, he later said that he attended school under a very severe master, but became quite skilled as a hawker and a horse rider.

His father died in 1501 and his mother sent him to Cambridge, where, in 1510, he became a Fellow of Jesus College. He had to forfeit his privileges as a Fellow when he married "Black Joan," a relative of the landlady of the Dolphin Inn, but he was reinstated after his wife died in childbirth. He was ordained in 1523, and graduated the following year.

He was given a position teaching divinity at Magdalen College, and also became an examiner for the University.

When the "sweating sickness" broke out in the summer of 1529, Cranmer determined to take two boys who were under his supervision back home to their parents in the county of Essex. By happenstance, he arrived in the town of Waltham, Essex, when Henry VIII was also there. While Cranmer was eating, he recognized Gardiner, the king's secretary, who was traveling with the king, and they began to talk. During the conversation he commented that if the university theologians decided that the king's marriage to Catherine of Aragon had been illegal in the first place, any ecclesiastical court would grant him a divorce. When the King heard this, he is reported as saying: "This man I trow, has got the right sow by the ear."

After an interview with the king at Greenwich, Cranmer was asked to write down his opinions, quoting the church fathers, scriptures and general councils which supported the argument. He was then promoted to the position of an archdeacon and subsequently was made one of the king's chaplains. He defended his views before the universities of Oxford and Cambridge, and in 1530 was dispatched to Rome to plead the king's case.

Failing at Rome, Cranmer was sent to Germany to air his views before the Lutheran princes. Also, and significantly, he was given political authority to lift certain trade embargoes, if he felt that would strengthen his cause. While he was there, he stayed with a gifted minister named Osiander, and in 1532 was secretly married to his niece. The marriage, though difficult to conceal, was dangerous to reveal, and was kept a secret for many years. On March 30 the following year, he was consecrated Archbishop of Canterbury.

We have already seen that it was Cranmer who declared Henry's marriage to Catherine to be "null and void," Cranmer who crowned Anne Queen—and Cranmer who, less than three years later, signed the papers for Henry's divorce from Anne. But above all, it was Cranmer who supervised the events of the Reformation. This was his most significant role. In 1538 the king commanded every parish church to buy an English Bible, and under Cranmer's influence the order was renewed in 1541. He stood almost alone in his opposition to Henry's Six Articles of 1539, which spelt out England's anti-Lutheran position, upholding the Roman doctrine of transubstantiation, and the celibacy of the priesthood. Though they were passed, despite his objections, and set Protestantism back, compliance with them was not rigidly enforced and the defeat proved to be temporary.

Cranmer was at Henry's bedside when he died. Henry VIII was never a Protestant at heart and he left a sum of £600 to pay for prayers to be said to shorten his time in purgatory.

Cranmer crowned Edward VI, shortening the ceremony because of the young king's frail health, and was at his bedside when he went out into eternity six years later. Others, seeing the dangers about to fall on Protestantism in England, fled to the continent, but Cranmer stayed beside Lady Jane Grey during her nine days on the throne.

Mary, who, as we have seen, seized the throne from Lady Jane Grey, was crowned in 1553. She vowed vengeance on Cranmer, whose views on Henry's divorce from her mother had made Mary illegitimate and who had helped to turn England towards the Protestant faith. Later that year he was taken to the Tower of London on the charge of treason. In September 1555, along with Ridley and Latimer, he was ordered to be tried, in his absence, by a papal commission sitting in Rome. In February 1556, when he was sixty-seven years old, he was stripped of his office by a special commission sent from Rome. It was at this time that he signed two recantations.

Because his position was second only to that of the monarch, and he had served as Archbishop of Canterbury for twenty-three years, Cranmer was given a specific day to make his recantation public. At St Mary's church, on March 21, 1556, to the shocked horror of his judges, he recanted his recantation. He held his right hand to the crowd and condemned it, promising that it would be the first part of his body to burn. With quiet confidence, he submitted himself to his fate. That day he held a meeting with Ridley, Latimer, Bilney and several other martyrs on the other side of Jordan.

The brain

John Frith was born in 1503 in Westerham, Kent, the son of Richard Frith, an inn-keeper. When he was a young man, he was sent to Cambridge, where he enrolled at the impressive King's College. It was there that he met Tyndale, who showed him how to find peace with God. He was a student of the classics, and was gifted with a brilliant mind and a photographic memory. He received his degree from Cambridge on December 7, 1525.

At that time Cardinal Wolsey was in the process of founding Cardinal College in Oxford (later to become Christ Church), and came to Cambridge in search of men qualified to become its foundation members. Cranmer, the future Archbishop of Canterbury, declined his offer, but Frith, with many others, accepted. He moved to Oxford and became a junior canon when the college opened in 1526.

It was in November 1527 that Bilney was arrested. At his trial in London, it came out that Thomas Garret had sold 350 books of Reformed theology on the black market. All of Bilney's known friends in Cambridge came under suspicion and were arrested. Frith's position was made more perilous when John Clark, an ex-Cambridge student and one of Frith's companions in Oxford, was found in his bedroom in Oxford reading his Bible to several other students. This led to the arrest of all Bilney's friends in Oxford, including Frith.

The group were imprisoned in a cave beneath the college, where salted fish was stored, and the experience killed three of them, including John Clark. At this point, Wolsey demanded the release of the rest. Some were made to carry faggots to the top of the Carfax intersection in Oxford, and burn a collection of forbidden books, but Frith managed to evade that punishment.

Frith escaped and fled across the Channel to Antwerp, where he met Tyndale, and a close friendship sprang up between the two men. Tyndale was one of Wolsey's intended victims, and Frith was able to strengthen Tyndale's resolve to stand firm. Stephen Vaughan, an English agent in Antwerp who had attempted to separate the two reformers, reported that John Frith had married, but nothing else is known about this.

Frith was out of England from 1528 to 1532, and during this time he wrote a number of books which were published in Antwerp. He became known for his forceful logic, his knowledge of the church fathers, and his forthright attack on Roman doctrines which needed reforming. The leaders of the opposition marked him down as a dangerous reformer and put a price on his head.

We are never told why, but Frith crossed the Channel back to England like a lamb wandering into a lion's lair. He made for the town of Reading, where the Prior was a friend of the reformers, holding Protestant services privately in his own home. But Frith was arrested for loitering before he could reach the prior's house. When he refused to give his name, he was put into stocks and held as a rogue and vagabond. Almost starving, he asked to see a schoolmaster named Cox, who managed to secure his release.

Frith then found that it was easier to get into England than to get out. He was again arrested at Southend, identified as a reformer, and sent to the Tower. Two secret reformers, Cromwell and Cranmer, held him as "a prisoner of the Crown," depriving his enemies of any opportunity to vent their hatred on him. This ensured his safety, within his captivity.

Five uneventful months elapsed. During this time Frith endeared himself to the jailor, and secured some privileges and liberties. A few people were permitted to visit him in prison, and on more than one occasion he was even given permission to leave his cell for a night. The jailor also allowed his friends to smuggle paper into and out of his cell. Those amenities secured for England the richest literature produced during the Reformation period. With the aid of the printing press, Frith was able to conduct a debate from his cell with no less an enemy of the Reformation than Sir Thomas More himself, the Chancellor of England. The papers were smuggled out of prison, published on the continent, and then circulated throughout England. Frith would write a challenge

Clare College, Cambridge, from the River Cam.

to More, and then reply to More's response. He quoted Ambrose, Chrysostom, Jerome, Tertullian, Origen and Athanasius—yet in his prison he did not have a single book. It was all entirely from memory. He was a controversialist *par excellence*.

Frith's writings on the Lord's Supper were powerful, clear, and effective. He was able to bring about the conversion of one of his opponents, and persuade other reformers that the subject of the Lord's Supper was serious—so serious that they should be willing to burn for what they believed. His arguments were later enshrined in the *Book of Common Prayer* of 1552.

Refusing many opportunities and encouragements to escape, Frith was tried at St Paul's on June 20, 1533, found guilty and imprisoned in Newgate to await execution. On July 4, 1533, he was taken to Smithfield and tied at the stake, back to back with a twenty-four-year-old tailor named Andrew Hewet. Though the wind blew the flames away from Frith, he smiled, knowing that, though it would prolong his suffering, it would quicken his friend's death. Frith had just turned thirty years of age when his spirit left his body at Smithfield.

The orator

John Frith debated the teaching of the Bible, Queen Anne Boleyn encouraged its circulation, and Hugh Latimer preached its message. He was probably born in 1485 at Thurcaston, only twelve miles from Lutterworth, where John Wycliffe had ministered. His father was a yeoman who rented his farm, and was earning "three or four pounds a year at the uttermost." To help his father, he looked after the five sheep and milked the thirty cows.

Latimer was enrolled as a student at Clare College, Cambridge, where he earned his B.A. degree in 1510, and his M.A. degree four years later. After that, he decided to study divinity. He worked hard and gained his degree in 1524. To graduate, he was required to deliver an oration on a religious subject, and selected for his topic a denunciation of Melanchthon, Luther's associate. His scathing criticisms of the German Reformation and the dexterity and skill with which they were delivered marked him out as a man of indisputable leadership gifts.

Latimer's mental prowess, along with his gift as an orator, were noticed by Thomas Bilney, who, as a Fellow of a college, was compelled to be present at the oration. As he listened, Bilney could visualize that gift being used in the cause of the Reformation. But Bilney was well-known as a heretic. How could he get a hearing with Latimer? When the applause had ended, and the congratulatory remarks were over, Bilney approached Latimer, and asked if he would hear his confession. In the confessional Bilney quoted very many passages of Scripture, and asked for his understanding of them to be corrected. Latimer listened for two hours, and then admitted that what Bilney had, he needed; and so another reformer was born.

When Latimer associated himself with the rădicals who met at the White Horse Inn, he provoked anger from the opposition. The Bishop of Ely forbade him to preach in the region of Cambridge; but, strangely, Cardinal Wolsey gave him freedom to preach anywhere in all England. In December 1529, he preached his two famous sermons entitled *Sermons on Cards*, in which he denounced card playing during the Christmas celebrations and suggested better employment with "Christ's cards," that is, His commandments.

The sermons caused turbulent controversy and attracted the king's attention. Latimer was invited to preach before Henry during Lent 1530, and that resulted in his appointment as a royal chaplain. Unlike others who addressed the king, Latimer was forthright. He reminded Henry that he was a mortal man, "having in you the corrupt nature of Adam . . . and no less needing the merits of Christ's passion." He even pictured the apostle Paul being forced to "carry faggots" to St Paul's for having declared, "Ye are not under law, but under grace."

John Stokesley, the Bishop of London, summoned Latimer to be examined by a board of bishops. This resulted in his excommunication and imprisonment. But the king intervened in Latimer's favor. The *Encyclopedia Britannica* comments: "It was, however, Latimer's preaching more than the edicts of Henry that established the principles of the Reformation in the minds and hearts of the people. His sermons are classics of their kind. Vivid, racy, terse in expression; profound in religious feeling, sagacious in their advice on human conduct. To the historical student they are of great value as a mirror of the social and political life of the period."

Latimer was consecrated Bishop of Winchester in 1535. Five years later, as bishop, he had the unpleasant task of preaching at the burning of John Forest, who had refused to acknowledge the king as head of the

Bishop Hugh Latimer, martyred at Oxford in 1555.

G. Vertue   *Sculpsit*

Church—this was required by the Six Articles of 1539. Latimer himself could not do this either, and so he resigned his bishopric, and was confined to the precincts of the palace belonging to the Bishop of Chichester. For the following seven years, he seems to have dropped out of sight. In 1546 he was brought before the Privy Council at Greenwich, and was again condemned and imprisoned at the Tower of London. By this time, Henry VIII had died, to be succeeded, as we have seen, by his only legitimate son, the young and sickly Edward VI, who strongly supported the

Protestant faith. Latimer was released and the House of Commons invited him to return to his see. In January of 1548 he resumed his preaching to larger crowds than ever.

In 1553, when Mary occupied the throne, he was summoned once more to appear before a council at Westminster. Though he could have escaped to the continent, he chose to attend, passing Smithfield on the way and commenting that it "groaned" for him. In 1554, he occupied a cell in the Tower with two good friends, Ridley, the Bishop of London, and Cranmer, the Archbishop of Canterbury. At their trial they were interrogated about the elements of the Lord's Supper and the propitiatory effects of the Mass. They were offered a final chance to recant, which neither Ridley nor Latimer accepted. On October 16, 1555, they were taken to the Oxford "town ditch" for execution on October 16, 1555. After listening to a sermon preached against them, they were tied to the stake and the faggots were lit. Latimer encouraged Ridley, saying, "Master Ridley, play the man. We shall this day light such a candle, by God's grace, in England, as I trust shall never be put out."

Latimer was seventy when his charred body, held up by chains, slumped over the embers. It was the "Indestructible Book" that changed his life, comforted him in distress, and from which he preached to others; and it changed England.

An engraving of the martyrdom of Nicholas Ridley and Hugh Latimer in Oxford, 1555.

The bridge builder

It is impossible to tell the story of the "Indestructible Book" without including the name of Thomas Cromwell. Many of his motives are questionable, but his involvement was fundamental to the success of reform in England. Without him, the story of the English Bible would have been significantly different. He was the bridge builder between the political and religious reforms.

Thomas Cromwell was probably born in 1485. His father Walter Cromwell, alias Smith, of Putney, was a drunken and dishonest brewer, blacksmith and fuller. After a quarrel, Thomas fled from his father's house, and it seems he went to Italy, where he joined the French army.

In December 1503, at the age of eighteen, he fought in the battle of Garigliano. From Italy he went to Florence and all we know is that he was befriended by a banker. When we next hear of him it is 1510 and he is in Antwerp, where he met a small group of Bostonians who were on their way to Rome seeking an indulgence from the pope to build a business guild in Boston. They hired Thomas to be their spokesman. He agreed, but before he addressed Pope Julius II he managed to present him with some candies from England. Permission for the guild was granted.

His next appearance is in London in 1512, when he married a well-to-do lady from Putney. By the early 1520s he was on the staff of the famous Cardinal Wolsey. By 1523 he became a Member of Parliament, and in 1524 was admitted to Grays Inn, one of the legal societies of London. His first speech in Parliament was on November 2, 1529, against the bill condemning Wolsey. The bill had already passed the House of Lords, and Wolsey was in serious trouble, but Cromwell's brilliant defense in the Commons turned the tide in Wolsey's favor. That speech brought Cromwell into the national spotlight. For the next decade, Cromwell was Henry's spokesman in Parliament, and Henry governed Parliament through Cromwell.

Cromwell was not the source of Henry's policy, but he was the instrument by which it was executed. The Reformation Acts which came between 1532 and 1539 were drafted by him. He was privy to all the off-the-record discussions, and dutifully reported them to the king. Cromwell's philosophy was clear. When Parliament considered independence from Rome, it was he who stated: "We have reflected upon the wants of the realm, and have come to the conclusion that the nation ought to form one body; that body can have but one head, and that head must be the king." Forming "one body" meant that the church must be an arm of the state, with the king as its head in place of the pope. As we have seen, good men on both sides of the Reformation divide suffered martyrdom for refusing to acknowledge this edict—men such as Sir Thomas More, and Bishop Fisher of Rochester. This Act of Parliament had unprecedented influence on the course to be followed by the church and the state, and Cromwell was the bridge between them.

In 1533 Cromwell became secretary to the king, in 1534 principal secretary and Master of the Rolls, and in 1536 keeper of the Privy Seal. He was the administrator responsible for effecting the king's decision to close down all monasteries in England, with the money from their sale going to the king. It was not the monks' immorality that drove him with such ruthless efficiency, but their submission to a foreign potentate in Rome. He was later rewarded by being made Earl of Essex, and his two associates were made secretaries to the king. Cromwell also centralized the administration of the country, so adding to his own importance.

But Cromwell over-played his hand, and the higher you go, the further there is to fall. His downfall was brought about by the changing

Thomas Cromwell, painted by Hans Holbein.

faces of international politics. Charles V and Francis I, two powerful rulers in Europe, totally committed to the Catholic faith, were planning to unite against Henry, and Cromwell devised a scheme to gain a counter-alliance with the Schmalkaldic League of German states. Henry was, at this time, between wives, and Princess Anne was available for marriage. She was the daughter of the Duke of Cleves, and sister-in-law to the Elector of Saxony. With the king's consent, Cromwell arranged the marriage. After great public fanfare, Anne of Cleves arrived in England, and was escorted to the king's palace at Greenwich. She turned out to be portly, ungainly, and ugly, lacking in grace and refinement. Henry was vastly disappointed, and although he felt he had to go through with the wedding for reasons of state, he never consummated the marriage.

The Anne of Cleves fiasco enabled Cromwell's enemies to turn

Henry against Cromwell. Henry struck at Cromwell remorselessly and suddenly, like a beast of prey. On June 10, 1540, six months after the arranged marriage, Henry accused Cromwell of treason, and sent him to the Tower. His ruthlessness and powerseeking had made him unpopular and a bill to have him executed was passed in Parliament, without a dissenting voice. He had not one friend left in the world, except perhaps for Cranmer. He lost his head by an axe on Tower Hill on June 20, 1540. He died attesting that he was a loyal and faithful adherent of the Catholic religion.

It must be said to Cromwell's credit that he was the principal instrument in making the Bible available to every Englishman, through every parish church in England. That fact cannot be overlooked, and will leave the church forever indebted to him. He also imposed the keeping of a register of births, deaths and marriages, and changed centuries of tradition by ordering certain parts of Anglican services to be recited in English instead of Latin.

Father of the English Bible

William Tyndale is in most respects "the father of the English Bible." It is true that Wycliffe's Bible preceded Tyndale's by 143 years, but it had never been printed. Moreover, since it had not been translated from the original languages but from the Latin Vulgate, it contained many errors. Erasmus' New Testament preceded Tyndale's by nine years, but it was in Greek and Latin, and only the academic world benefited. While Erasmus desired, according to the preface of his New Testament, "that the ploughman would sing a text of Scripture at his plough," he did not make it possible, unless the ploughman was educated in Greek. It was Tyndale who provided the Bible in the laborer's language.

William Tyndale was born near the Welsh border in the early 1490s. Nothing is known about his parents, or his brothers John and Edward. He became a student at Magdalen Hall in Oxford, and graduated with his Master's degree in 1515. He left Oxford for Cambridge and may have become associated with Bilney's White Horse Inn fellowship which was to produce archbishops, bishops and martyrs. It was here in Cambridge that Tyndale witnessed the spellbinding and regenerating power of the Word of God.

Tyndale realized that only the barriers of culture prevented revival spreading beyond Cambridge and decided that if the ordinary man cannot step up to where he can understand the Bible, then the Bible must step down. Thus he was fired with the vision of translating the Bible into the language of the common man. It became the task of his life and the cause of his death.

Tyndale left Cambridge in 1521 for Little Sodbury Manor, near the city of Bristol, where he worked for Sir John Walsh, probably as tutor to

Statue of William Tyndale in Embankment Gardens, London.

his children. He spent his spare time preaching in the neighborhood, and in his small attic room he started on the work of translating the Bible. But this was a dangerous occupation. Back in 1408 a law had been passed against the Lollards, forbidding any use of Scripture that was not in Latin. Just two years before Tyndale started his task, six men and one woman had been burned to death in Coventry for teaching their children to recite the Lord's Prayer in English. Tyndale was endangering the lives of the Walsh family by translating the Bible under their roof.

Tyndale knew it was within the power of the Bishop of London, Cuthbert Tunstall, to give him a job in his household translating the Bible, so he left Little Sodbury for London, but it soon became clear that neither in London nor in all England would he receive the permission he needed. Tyndale was determined to translate the Bible into English

Opposite: **The towering Cologne Cathedral, Germany. Tyndale found temporary refuge—and a printer—in Cologne.**

no matter what the cost, and he decided to exile himself from his native land. He spent six months working for a merchant who was involved in subsidizing and importing forbidden Protestant books, and then set sail for the continent, never to see his homeland again.

The translation was finished in Wittenberg, Luther's town. Though Luther was ten years Tyndale's senior, and they did not agree on all interpretations of Scripture, they were strongly united by the motto "sola scriptura"—the Scriptures alone. While he was in Wittenberg, Tyndale enrolled at the university under an assumed name and became friends with William Roy, a fellow Englishman, who assisted him with the writing and promised to help him get the manuscript published.

The printing was the most difficult task of all. They went to Cologne, where they found a willing printer, but English spies broke up the operation. As the spies came in through the front door Tyndale was escaping through the back door with whatever copies were finished. It was a narrow escape. If he had been found it would almost certainly have meant imprisonment and death. The two men traveled to Worms, where they found Peter Schoeffer, a printer who was willing to complete the task. The Bibles were ready for shipping in December, 1525, and Tyndale and Roy parted company, the goal of their partnership achieved.

The Bibles reached England in the spring of 1526 and fomented national unrest. The king condemned them to a public burning and harassed and persecuted all found guilty of possessing or distributing them. The story is told that Tunstall authorized a merchant trading in Antwerp to buy every available volume and bring them back to London for burning. What Tunstall did not know was that the merchant was Tyndale's friend, and at the king's expense paid Tyndale four times the cost of production for each copy. So, for every Bible Tunstall burned, the king paid for three more to be added to Tyndale's arsenal.

There was now a price on Tyndale's head. Bounty hunters from England began traveling all over the continent, wearing disguises, paying for information and tracking down leads, but all without success. They would bump into each other—but not into Tyndale! Not one of them had the slightest knowledge of his whereabouts. Tyndale moved to Marburg and, in disguise, started to study Hebrew so that he might begin the translation of the Old Testament. Having mastered this language, he moved to Hamburg, and from there to Antwerp. It was at this point that he influenced both John Frith and Miles Coverdale. Frith was to die by burning at Smithfield, but Coverdale survived to play a major part in the translation and publication of the Bible in English.

For the next few years, Tyndale must have known how a fox feels when the countryside is surrounded by hounds in the hunt. He became a fugitive, wandering in various disguises from city to city. What made him particularly elusive was his mastery of seven languages, each of which he spoke like a native.

Indelible ink

The difficulties of life on the run were not the only pressures on Tyndale. He also had the pressure of his exacting translation work. "Scripture derives its authority from him who sent it," he stated, and he never deviated from this conviction that he was translating the inspired Word of God. Such a task demanded the utmost care, no matter how adverse the conditions. Foxe reports that Tyndale would say: "I call God to record that I have never altered, against the voice of my conscience, one syllable of his Word. Nor would do this day, if all the pleasures, honours, and riches of the earth might be given me."

A further pressure was the burden to complete his task. When he had translated the Pentateuch, he traveled from Antwerp to Hamburg by ship. On the voyage, a fierce storm wrecked the ship and everything was lost, including his precious manuscripts and his money. He had lost many hours' work. When he eventually arrived in Hamburg, Miles Coverdale met him there, and between April and December 1529 they worked together on the translation of the five books of Moses. Early in 1530, the first publication of Tyndale's Pentateuch came off the presses. By the time of his capture, he had finished translating up to 2 Chronicles and the book of Jonah. He was never able to complete the rest of the Old Testament, but, inspired by his vision, others completed it on his behalf.

It might be assumed that a man of such indomitable commitment would have no time for anything else, but Tyndale wrote other books dealing with the issues of the Reformation. In 1528 he wrote two which were to become standards for the reform movement. The first was *The Parable of the Wicked Mammon*, and the second was *The Obedience of a Christian Man*. These two books defended two significant principles: the authority of the Bible in the church, and the supremacy of the king in the state. They were followed two years later by another publication, *The Practice of Prelates*, which was a strong indictment against the Roman Catholic Church and the divorce of Henry VIII. These became well known and influential in England. A martyr named Tewkesbury was put to the body rack at the Tower of London because he refused to renounce the teaching in *Wicked Mammon*. He testified that this book had introduced him to Christ.

1529 was the year of one of Tyndale's most famous controversies. Thomas More had written his *Dialogue of Sir Thomas More, touching the Pestilent Sect of Luther and Tyndale*, and as More was considered the leading English defender of the Church of Rome, Tyndale picked up his pen to reply. The dispute which followed dealt with all the arguments for and against the Reformation, and centered on whether the church or Scripture held the higher authority. C. S. Lewis described the debate as a "great Platonic dialogue, perhaps the best specimen of that form ever produced in English." Some of Tyndale's strongest critics

Bibles imported from Europe are burned at the bishop's instruction.

complimented him on his skill, and Erasmus, one of More's closest friends, wrote to Tunstall, the Bishop of London, admitting, "I cannot heartily congratulate More."

Tyndale found refuge for some time in the city of Antwerp, where he may have stayed at the home of Thomas Poyntz, a relative of Mrs Walsh from Little Sodbury Manor. Here he worked on his translations, and edited his previous publications. He was unable to stay and supervise a new edition of his New Testament, which was published in 1534, "full of printing errors." He returned in 1535 to the same home, where he met Henry Phillips, a man to whom the family had shown much kindness, and who professed to be a student of the new faith. It was Phillips who betrayed the identity of the reformer. He borrowed forty shillings from Tyndale and, going out to dine, pointed him out to the men lying in wait. On May 24, 1535, Tyndale was captured and taken to the impregnable Vilvorde Castle near Brussels, in Belgium.

When he was tried, Tyndale rejected the offer of counsel. He deemed his judges to be both prejudiced and bitter, and felt that the outcome was already decided. His counsel would merely have argued over issues of no real consequence, but he himself could bear witness to the truth of the gospel. He did not want to defend himself, but he did want to defend his Bible. He was found guilty of sacrilege, dressed in his sacerdotal robes and brought before the bishop. The bishop pronounced him excommunicated, had the official robes taken from him, and had a barber shave his head; then he was taken back to his cell.

William Tyndale is burned at the stake in Flanders.

It was not until September or October 1536 that his executioners brought him out to be killed. They chained him to a pillar with two holes in it, through which they threaded a piece of wire in order that, according to his sentence, he might be strangled as well as burned. Tyndale showed no fear, regret or hesitation. When the executioner was attaching the wire around his throat, he made his last recorded comment. It was a prayer: "Lord, open the king of England's eyes."

They strangled his voice. They burned his hands. They ravaged and destroyed his property, burning every Bible they could find. But their efforts to silence him failed. Though only one copy of the first edition of his New Testament survived the biblical holocaust, his commitment inspired thousands, his priorities gave guidance to the movement, and his translation influenced nearly every succeeding translation of the Bible.

The Bishop of Exeter

Another young man who came through that unique Bible study group at the White Horse Inn in Cambridge was Miles Coverdale. He was born in Yorkshire in 1488, was ordained priest at Norwich in 1514, and entered the convent of Augustinian friars at Cambridge, where he studied philosophy and theology. While there he made the acquaintance of Sir Thomas More, and in More's home he met Thomas Cromwell, the future Chancellor of England. The prior of his abbey was Robert Barnes, who was converted under the ministry of Thomas Bilney. Barnes introduced Coverdale to the study of the scriptures, and this eventually led him to participate in the disputes at the White Horse Inn. When his prior was arrested, and placed on trial in London, Coverdale went to give him legal assistance.

Miles Coverdale, translator of the English Bible.

Coverdale later left the friary, abandoning his vows to become an itinerant preacher. He traveled considerably, especially on the continent. He was in Hamburg in 1529, where, as we have seen, he aided Tyndale in his translation of the Pentateuch, though it is difficult to know what assistance he gave, since as far as we can tell he had no knowledge of the Hebrew language. At the same time, he started his own writing career. Most of his twenty-six publications were English translations of reformed writers.

Jacob van Meteren, an Antwerp merchant, hired him to produce an English translation of the Bible, a task he completed in 1535. When his fellow clergy argued for the retention of the Scriptures in Latin, he said: "No, the Holy Ghost is as much the author of it in Hebrew, Greek, French, Dutch, and English, as in Latin."

The first edition of this, the first Bible to be printed in English, appeared on October 4, 1535. There are no complete copies in existence, and on the five or six fragments which have a title page there is no indication of the publisher or the place of its publication. In order to make his translation more acceptable in England, Coverdale dedicated it to the king and to "his dearest just wife, and most virtuous princess, Queen Anne." But when Anne was disgraced and executed a few months later, this dedication became a liability.

In December 1534, Coverdale had attended a Convocation called by Archbishop Cranmer, which petitioned for an authorized translation of the scriptures in English. Coverdale now wanted to have his edition authorized, but this attempt failed. The version was not even particularly scholarly. Some of the title pages state that it was translated out of German and Latin but Coverdale admitted to using five translations—two Latin, two German (Luther's and the Zurich Bible), and Tyndale's New Testament and Pentateuch. Two fresh editions appeared in 1537, but none received official approval; in fact, in 1542 Coverdale's Bible was placed on a list of banned books.

Coverdale was in Geneva in December 1538, and participated in the preparation of the Geneva Bible. But his greatest accomplishment in the history of the English Bible was yet ahead of him. This came in 1539 when Thomas Cromwell commissioned him to edit the Matthew Bible, giving England its greatest authorized version of Henry's reign.

Apart from his work on the Bible, Coverdale contributed to the reform movement by offering support and help in many ways. First, though the Six Articles condemned marriage among priests, Coverdale defied this law by openly marrying Elizabeth Machson. Second, he was staying at Windsor Castle in October 1548 when Cranmer was drawing up the First Book of Common Prayer, and he helped in that task. Third, he was active in many of the reforming measures of the reign of Edward VI. Fourth, as Bishop of Exeter, a position he held from 1551 to 1553, he was in constant attendance at the Parliaments. Fifth, he was an aggressive persecutor of the anabaptist movement, which at that time was considered detrimental to the reformers' cause. Finally, and most important, he was an exceptionally gifted preacher. (On one significant occasion, he preached at St Paul's on the second Sunday of Lent to mark the ceremonial abolition of multiple altars and masses, and his sermon was immediately followed by the pulling down of the high altar.)

Coverdale lost his bishopric when Mary came to the throne in 1553. He was required to stand before the Privy Council but was spared burning by the intercession in his favor of Christian III of Denmark, and was allowed to go to the continent "with two of his servants" (one of whom was his wife!). He returned to England when Elizabeth ascended the throne in 1558 and ministered in the area of London Bridge, always attracting large crowds. He died in February 1568, and is buried in the graveyard at St Magnus Church.

Mary's first victim

While it is contended by some that "Matthew" was merely a harmless pen name attached to a Bible translation, it would be more accurate to say that the name was used in a deliberate attempt to deceive the authorities, and get the book distributed on the black market. While Tyndale also broke the law by distributing an undercover Bible, he did not use a false name. The Matthew Bible, as it came to be known, is directly traced to John Rogers.

Rogers was born near the city of Birmingham about the year 1500. He was educated at Pembroke Hall, in Cambridge, and in 1526 graduated with a B.A. degree, apparently unmoved by the spiritual stirring which affected the university during his student days. In 1532 he became rector of Holy Trinity, Queenhithe, in London. Two years later, he accepted the post of chaplain to the English merchants who traded in Antwerp. It was there that he came into contact with William Tyndale.

Tyndale had a profound effect upon Rogers, though their friendship was very brief. The change in Rogers' life was evidenced by his desertion of the Catholic Church; by his marriage to a woman from Antwerp; and by the fact that Tyndale trusted him so implicitly that he left all his unpublished translations in his possession for safe keeping. Tyndale had already translated the Old Testament as far as 2 Chronicles, but nothing had been published since the Pentateuch. The translation had to be finished and the complete Bible published.

It is questionable whether John Rogers knew enough Hebrew to complete the translating work. The similarity of the second half of the Old Testament to that of Coverdale's Bible seems to indicate that Coverdale helped to supervise the finishing of the Old Testament. It seems there was a deliberate subterfuge, and that Tyndale's translation was edited in order to conceal the source. The completed Bible, under the pseudonym of Thomas Matthew, was published in 1537, just one year after Tyndale's death.

The manuscripts were given for publication to Richard Grafton, a merchant in Antwerp who felt constrained to go to England and present a copy to Cranmer, the Archbishop of Canterbury, in an effort to get approval for an English publication. Cranmer examined the book and was greatly impressed, but he felt he was not the best person to obtain the king's approval. He therefore asked Thomas Cromwell to submit it and obtain permission from Henry VIII. The permission he was asking for was temporary: it was to be only until a better translation could be produced by the bishops—which, suggested Cranmer, "will not be till a day after domesday." The king took the book and looked through it. At the end of Malachi, Rogers had etched the initials W.T., standing for William Tyndale. The letters were large enough to cover half the page, but either the King's fingers skipped the page, or he did not look at the initials properly, or his mind was too dull to interpret their significance; as far as he could see, Tyndale's name was not associated with the new Bible. The book had a pleasant dedication to His Majesty, and Henry thought that it might be a useful implement to weaken the grip of Rome on England. He handed it back to Cromwell and granted permission, provided Cromwell could get Cranmer's approval! Cromwell had succeeded, and an edition of 1,500 copies was sold in England as the first "authorized" version. According to its title page, it was published "by the king's most gracious licence."

This was a red-letter day in the history of the English Bible. Though the Matthew Bible was not to survive for long, it paved the way for later editions and translations. It succeeded where Coverdale's had failed, in obtaining the king's authorization.

For several years Rogers was the pastor of a Protestant congregation in Wittenberg, returning to England in 1548. In 1550 he ministered at two churches in London, and the following year he was made a prebendary of St Paul's. After a brief examination of his gifts, he was made a lecturer in divinity.

When Mary became sovereign, many of the leaders of the Reformation fled to the continent, but Rogers was obstinate, determined and a fully committed reformer. On July 27, 1553, he preached at St Paul's on "the true doctrine taught in King Edward's days" and warned his congregation against any going back to "pestilent Popery." Ten days later he was placed under house arrest.

In January 1554, Bonner, the new Bishop of London, sent Rogers to Newgate, where he was imprisoned with John Hooper and John Bradford. He was confined in Newgate for twelve months until January 22, 1555, and then was brought to the home of Gardiner, the notorious persecutor of the reformers. Six days later he had to face a commission appointed by Cardinal Pole, at which Gardiner sentenced him to death

Bishop Edward Bonner, persecutor of the English Protestants.

for denying the Christian character of the Church of Rome and refusing to accept that the elements at the Lord's Supper turned into the actual body and blood of Christ. Six days later, on February 4, 1555, he was taken to Smithfield and was burned to death, the first Christian martyr during the reign of Mary. His fellow prisoner, Bradford, said "he broke the ice valiantly."

Chains of freedom

The Matthew Bible, which was growing in popularity, had many strongly anti-Catholic footnotes. Since the edition had official approval, these were something of an embarrassment to Cromwell when he was handling delicate foreign affairs involving Catholic countries. Cromwell therefore decided that another Bible must replace the Matthew version.

Having obtained the king's permission, Cromwell commissioned Coverdale and the publisher Richard Grafton to revise the Matthew text and eliminate the footnotes. To speed the operation and improve the quality of production, Cromwell arrannged for it to be printed in Paris, where there was finer paper and a superior printing press. Charles I of France agreed, since it would be in a language his people did not understand and would immediately be shipped out of France. At the end of

Opposite: Title page of the Coverdale Bible, which first appeared in 1535, and was dedicated to King Henry VIII.

spring, 1538, Coverdale and his assistant arrived in Paris, selecting François Regnault as printer.

On December 13 Coverdale and Grafton, who were worried about a resurgence in the activities of the Inquisition, persuaded the English ambassador, Bonner, to take most of the completed pages to Cromwell. Whether because of the Inquisition or because Charles had changed his mind, work stopped, and four days later the revisers had to flee for their lives. The pages they had to leave behind were condemned to be burned in the Place Maulbert. However, a haberdasher who was an English agent bought some on the pretext that he needed the paper to stuff his hats, and other agents, working at night in cloak and dagger style, stole the presses and all the type and even the printers, and transported them all to London. In April 1539 the whole Bible was finished, and the editors added the words: "To the Lord the achievement is due."

Because the work was undertaken under royal patronage, there was no dedication. The 9 x 15–inch pages had no footnotes. The title page was a wood engraving, artistically created by Holbein, which eloquently told the story of royal supremacy. The Bible was given to the public not by the church but by the king, and was distributed through the priests to the people.

The title page reads: "The Byble in Englyshe, that is to saye the content of all the Holy Scrypture, bothe of ye Olde and Newe Testament, truly translated after the veryte of the Hebrue and Greke Textes, by ye dylygent studye of dyuerse excellent learned men, expert in theforsayde tongues. Prynted by Rychard Graftoni & Edward Whitchurch . . . 1539."

Within two years, 20,000 copies had been sold (rendering obsolete another version of the Matthew Bible with softened footnotes, which the Oxford scholar Richard Taverner had published in 1539). Cranmer passed the verdict that it contained "no heresies," and a royal declaration commanded it to be bought by every parish church in the land and made accessible on a reading desk for the public to read at any time. Readers had to be provided for those who could not read it themselves. Bible reading, which had once been forbidden, then silently tolerated, then licenced, was now commanded, and for this we are indebted to Thomas Cromwell.

Because of its bulk, the new Bible came to be known as the Great Bible. It is also sometimes called the Chained Bible, because copies were chained to the reading desks, or Cranmer's Bible, because of an elaborate preface which Cranmer added to the second edition in 1540. By the end of 1541 there were no fewer than seven editions.

Based as it was on the Matthew Bible, which in turn had been based on Tyndale, this stands as Tyndale's memorial. The Great Bible remained the English Bible for twenty years. Tyndale had burned to ashes in a foreign land, but the Great Bible was in every respect the fruit of his labor and the memorial of his life.

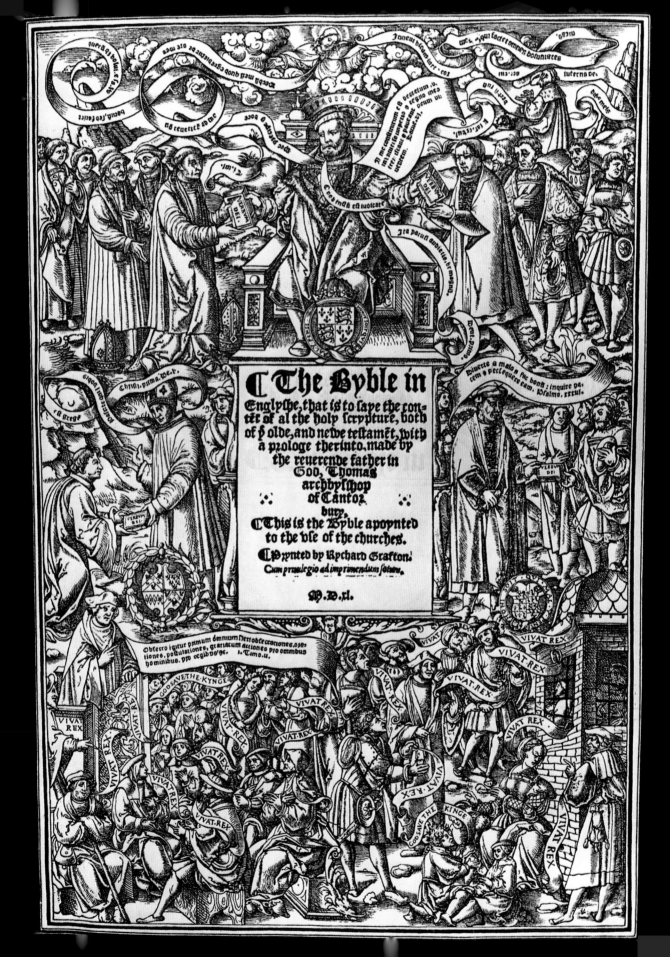

Committee work

It seems odd that an English Bible should have the word Geneva in its title, yet that is what happened. Here is the story behind it. In 1543 an Act of Parliament for the "Advancement of True Religion," took away permission for the use of any Bible other than the Great Bible. The Act specifically outlawed the writings of Tyndale, and a later Act added Wycliffe and Coverdale. Tyndale's Bible was "clearly and utterly abolished and forbidden to be kept or used." But Henry VIII died on January 28, 1547, and the young Edward VI's coronation brought a reversal of attitude. At his coronation, when he was given the three swords symbolizing the countries under his dominion, he asked the whereabouts of the fourth. His nobles asked him what he meant. "The Bible," he responded, "the sword of the Spirit, and to be preferred before these swords." During Edward's reign, there were at least thirteen editions of the whole Bible and thirty-five of the New Testament. It was during his reign that the Book of Common Prayer was introduced, and the Church of England's doctrinal standard appeared in the *Forty-Two Articles*, later to be reduced to the *Thirty-Nine Articles*.

But as we have seen, "Bloody Mary" came to the throne in July 1553 and her husband, Philip II of Spain, was a fanatical champion of the Inquisition. When Mary forbade the public use of Scripture, a migration to Europe began, especially to Calvin's city; deans and bishops of England and Scotland, including Miles Coverdale and Scotland's John Knox, made a European London out of Geneva.

Whittingham's New Testament

A new translation of the New Testament in English came out of Geneva in 1557. It was the work of one man, William Whittingham, who was married to Calvin's sister-in-law and who succeeded Knox in the pastorate of the English congregation in Geneva in 1559. His New Testament was a revision of Tyndale's, with an introduction written by Calvin, and was addressed to "simple lambs which partly are already in the fold . . . and partly wandering, through ignorance." It aimed to use everyday Anglo-Saxon language rather than literary words derived from Latin. Thus a parable was a "biword," regeneration was "gainbirth," and crucified became "crossed."

Whittingham's New Testament had two unique features. First, it used verse divisions for the first time in an English Bible. While traveling between Paris and Lyons in 1551, the printer Robert Estienne had hastily marked up the verses for one of his editions of the Greek Testament. Some of his divisions are questionable: "I think it had been better done on his knees in a closet," said one Bible historian. But though these divisions are criticized, they remain in universal use.

Whittingham's second innovation was the use of different type to indicate words added in translation which are not in the original text—a practice which was to be followed by the King James version of 1611. So extensive are Whittingham's analyses and notes that the edition has been called "the first critical edition of the New Testament in English."

While the reformers in Geneva waited for political change to come at home, they "could think of nothing which could be more acceptable to God, and as comfortable to His Church, than in the translating of the Scriptures into our native tongue." The Bible they produced was called the *Geneva Bible*, and was printed in 1560.

Geneva Bible

The group who produced the Geneva Bible included John Knox, Miles Coverdale, William Whittingham and other less well known authorities. They were, to use their own description, "so many godly and learned men." John Calvin and Theodore Beza were at hand when they needed scholarly help, and they had access to other translations in several foreign languages. In fact, their source material was greater than that afforded to any previous translator. They painstakingly worked over every minute detail of the text, giving a faithful translation and achieving agreement between all the collaborators. They prided themselves on their accomplishment: the text proved to be so good that a complete revision was never needed, and the method of translation worked so well that it was later adopted by the committees who worked on the King James Version.

The Bible became known as the Breeches Bible because of its translation of Genesis 3:7, which says that Adam and Eve sowed fig leaves into "breeches." The translators also included marginal readings. Though some were biased in favor of Calvin's theology, and some were strongly anti-papal, the majority were simply explanatory notes. The Bible was intended for personal use rather than for reading in church and therefore it was issued in a moderate quarto format which made it easier to carry.

Though it was never sanctioned for public use in England, its convenient size quickly made the Geneva Bible the "household" Bible. When the 1644 edition appeared in England, thirty-three years after the publication of the Authorized Version, it had already passed through more than 140 editions. It was particularly the puritans' Bible, and became the Bible of the Commonwealth army. Soldiers did not carry a full Bible, but they did have a pocket-sized reader, which quoted from the Geneva version. It was the Bible exclusively used by the Pilgrim Fathers. The Geneva text was also used for the first Bible printed in Scotland, named the Bassandyne Bible after its printer (1679). Parliament required every householder having a certain income to possess a copy. In June, 1580, a man called John Williamson was commissioned to visit and search every house, "and to require sight of their Bible and Psalm-book, if they have one, to be marked with their own name." The name was to stop anyone trying to get away with borrowing a copy from a neighbor!

The Bishops' Bible

As Elizabeth's coronation procession wound its way through the streets of London, a man appeared with a scythe and wings, representing Father Time, leading his daughter, representing Truth. She carried an English Bible, bearing the inscription *The Word of Truth*, and presented it to Her Majesty. Queen Elizabeth graciously received it and pressed it to her breast, having promised that she would "oftentimes read over that book."

In 1559 Elizabeth pleased her citizens by originating an Act, as Edward VI had done before her, which stated that "one book of the whole Bible of the largest volume in English" should be set up in every parish. The following year she allowed an English printing of the Geneva Bible to be dedicated to her.

The next Reformation Bible appeared in 1586. Sometimes called the fourth revision of the Tyndale translation, it came into existence through the insistence of Matthew Parker. He had been Anne Boleyn's chaplain, and by 1544 had been elected the master of Corpus Christi College, at the recommendation of Henry VIII. When Anne Boleyn was executed, she surrendered her young daughter Elizabeth to his care; and on August 1, 1559, Elizabeth, now the reigning queen, appointed him Archbishop of Canterbury.

Parker believed that a new Bible was needed because the success of the Geneva Bible not only undermined the prestige of the Great Bible, England's official Bible, but also weakened the authority of the bishops. In 1564, he organized a committee of some eight or nine bishops whom he considered to be the bestqualified men among the clergy, and they determined to make another revision of the Great Bible, re-establishing its prestige. Their revision became known as the Bishops' Bible.

Parker divided "the whole Bible in to parcels," and told his translators to "peruse and collate" the text. They were, he said, to "follow the common English translation used in the churches, and not recede from it, but where it varieth manifestly from the Hebrew or Greek original." They were to "make no bitter notes upon any text," nor were they allowed to "set down any determination in places of controversy."

The bishops' version followed the Great Bible in the historical sections, but elsewhere it showed the distinct influence of the Geneva Bible. Some scholars contend that the translators purposely limited the number of times they used the Geneva version—after all, they could not show too much indebtedness to the very version they were attempting to replace. It was claimed by others that this reduced its accuracy. The 1574 version marked certain passages in "places not edifying . . . so that the reader may eschew them in his public reading."

To improve the quality of the production, the thickest paper was used, together with the best printing facilities available. The Bible

included a number of woodcuts, a description of the Holy Land, and a chart of St Paul's journeys. The front page contained the simple title, *The Holie Bible*, with the words of Romans 1:16 written in Latin beneath the title. The title page had an engraving of Elizabeth, and there were portraits of the Earl of Leicester and the Earl of Cecil at the beginning of the Book of Joshua and the Book of Psalms.

Its many woodcuts made the book costly and cumbersome. Moreover, scholars did not find the translation satisfying. Different sections were translated in a variety of styles by scholars from different fields of study, and nobody attempted to co-ordinate and harmonize the finished product.

The English Bible: Chronology

THE BIBLE IN MANUSCRIPT

1384 Wycliffe's translation (from the Latin)
1396 Purvey's revision

THE BIBLE IN PRINT

1525 Tyndale's New Testament
1530 Tyndale's Old Testament
1534 Tyndale's New Testament (revised)
1535 Coverdale's Bible (from the Latin, Luther and Zwingli)
1537 Matthew (based on Tyndale)
1539 Taverner's revision (based on Matthew)
1539 Great Bible (based on Matthew)
1557 Whittingham's New Testament
1560 Geneva Bible
1568 Bishops' Bible
1582 Rheims New Testament (based on Latin)
1610 Douai Bible (Old Testament based on Latin)
1611 Authorized Version
1881 Revised New Testament
1885 Revised Old Testament
1901 American Revision (of the Revised Version)

Parker assumed that he would obtain royal favour for his efforts. On October 5, 1568, a copy of the completed translation was ready for presentation to the queen. It was to be presented by Sir William Cecil, Secretary of State, and Parker wrote to ask him to get the queen to licence it as the sole edition for public reading in churches. This, he said, would achieve uniformity. But despite the favor Parker enjoyed with Elizabeth, she never granted him his desire. The Constitutions and Canons of 1571 stated that "Every archbishop and bishop should have at his house a copy of the Holy Bible of the largest volume, as lately printed in London." But the Bible referred to here was the Great Bible. The decree of 1573 that the Bishops' Bible should be read publicly in the churches came from Parker himself, without royal authority.

The Bishops' Bible was never officially accepted. Though it survived for forty years, and went through twenty editions, the last being in 1606, it was considered to be the weakest of all the Reformation Bibles.

6. The Bible in England and America

The Elizabethan pests

When Elizabeth came to the throne, the Catholic policies of Mary were abruptly ended. During the unstable and uncertain period before Elizabeth had established her authority, she faced two threats from abroad; both threats were of a religious nature, and they came from opposite extremes.

One was the Catholic threat. Philip II of Spain and the pope wanted to see the restoration of Catholicism in England, and many influential families would have welcomed another Catholic monarch. However the threat of her overthrow increased popular support for her.

The second threat came from Englishmen who had fled to the continent from the fury of Queen Mary. When they returned, they called for a stricter morality, for a reformed theology and for new policies in church government. The characteristics of this movement were, first, that it originated in Geneva. Strongly influenced as they were by Luther, Calvin and other reformers, these returning exiles were dissatisfied with the Church of England's practices in baptism and the communion service. They also upheld Calvinist ideas of church government which were based on the primacy of the church over the state, and the rule of a body of presbyters rather than individual bishops. Every attempt was made to find a compromise between episcopacy and presbyterianism, but they were fundamentally incompatible. Moreover Elizabeth saw any attack on the power of bishops—even from Parliament—as a threat to the monarchy itself. She felt that if the laity could dictate to a bishop, they would soon start dictating to her!

Second, this strongly Protestant outlook soon dominated the academic world. Works of Reformed theology began pouring off the presses. Cambridge had already been flooded with underground publications, and now Calvin's works, especially his *Institutes of the Christian Religion*, became, in effect, textbooks for a rising generation of

Opposite: Queen Elizabeth I, by an unknown artist.

Cambridge-trained clergymen. By the middle of Elizabeth's reign the position was the same in Oxford. Since all theologians and preachers studied at Oxford or Cambridge, Protestant ideas soon dominated the pulpits of England.

Third, Protestant thinking also infiltrated the homes. As we have seen, the officially approved Great Bible (and later the Bishops' Bible) were intended for use in church, and attempted to influence the nation through the church, but the Geneva Bible, smaller and cheaper, was the Bible that was found in people's homes. Its notes and comments brought the influence of Calvinistic theology straight to the people, bypassing pulpits and thus diminishing the sovereign's control over the minds of her subjects.

The movement for reform gained ground within the Church of England and threatened Elizabeth's control over the Church. Its adherents, dubbed "Puritans," were angered by anything that savored of Roman Catholicism—the wearing of vestments (in fact, the use of any distinctive clerical dress at all); kneeling at the reception of the holy communion; the ceremony of the ring at weddings; and the sign of the cross at baptism. But when the Puritans pressed for the abolition of these things, Elizabeth turned a deaf ear to their arguments.

In 1570, Pope Pius V published a Bull of excommunication and deposition against Elizabeth, and asked the French and the Spanish to carry it out. It was akin to a declaration of war against the Queen, and it called for all Catholics to resist her authority. From 1574 to 1581, Catholic missionaries poured into England from France. The Society of Jesus, known as the Jesuits, entered the fray, planning to place Mary Queen of Scots on the throne and assassinate Elizabeth. This called for drastic measures. An oath of allegiance was imposed on all known Roman Catholics, and on all suspected of disloyalty. Anyone who denied the queen's right to the throne was guilty of high treason. This turned the tables on the pope, and forced his subjects to deny his authority, at peril of their lives. From 1571 to 1606, a series of statues were passed which not only denied religious liberty to Catholics, but also robbed them of the ordinary rights of citizens. About 200 Roman Catholics, including clergy, laymen and women, were executed. It strengthened the Elizabethan grip on the church, and this in turn frustrated puritan ambitions.

Puritans who were dissatisfied with the established church now fell into two groups: those who wanted to see Church of England reformation carried further; and the independents, or separatists, who saw no possibility of satisfaction in the Church of England and sought freedom to worship in their own independently organized churches.

In the late 1580s and early 1590s there was a fresh outbreak of hostility to the establishment following the publication of tracts by the fictitious "Martin Marprelate." These called bishops "incarnate devils" and

the Archbishop of Canterbury "the Beelzebub of Canterbury" or the "Canterbury Caiaphas." The group of extreme Puritans, among whom these tracts had originated, were led by Thomas Cartwright (c1535–1603). Some went to prison rather than take the oath of loyalty which had been designed for Catholics.

Catholic response

It was clear even to the Catholic faithful of Europe that renewal was necessary in the Catholic Church. As part of that movement, later to be known as the Counter-Reformation, the great Council of Trent was held at Trent in Italy. It met in three sessions between 1545 and 1563. It had been summoned to deal with the unity of the church (which the emperor Charles V and others saw as inseparable from political unity), and to define dogma.

The Council was adamant on the use of the Bible by the laity: "The Holy Scriptures, though truly and Catholikely translated into vulgar tongues, may not be indifferently read of all men, nor by any other than such as have express license thereunto of their lawful ordinaries, with good testimony from their curates and confessors that they be humble, discreet, and devote persons, and like to take much good and no harm thereby." In other words, to buy a Bible required a license from the priest, and to read it required an admission in the confessional.

But Protestants were becoming familiar with their Bible in their own language, and were quoting it in defence of their doctrine. Catholics needed to be equipped to answer them, and Catholics in England needed an English translation of their own instead of reading versions which incorporated Protestant interpretations.

Just as there had been a migration of reformers from England when Mary Tudor came to the throne, so there was a migration of Catholics at the appearance of Queen Elizabeth. The three men who were responsible for the Catholic translation were all refugees from Oxford. The chief among them was William Allen, a distinguished priest who was canon of York during the reign of Mary. It is believed that if the Spanish Armada had succeeded Willam Allen would have been nominated Primate of all England.

In 1568 Allen had gone to Douai, in France, where Philip II of Spain had founded a university a few years earlier. Here he determined to build a college for the training of English Catholics—there were already Irish and Scottish colleges, preparing priests for an immediate takeover in England, should the opportunity present itself again. Allen encouraged Gregory Martin, who knew both Greek and Hebrew, to do the translating. In turn, Martin involved Robert Bristow, who was the main contributor of the marginal and foot notes.

In 1578, a political disturbance required Allen to move the college from Douai to Rheims, and in 1593, for similar reasons, to move it back to Douai. There was a space of nearly twenty-eight years between the publication of the two Testaments. The New Testament was completed and published in 1582, from Rheims. The Old Testament was not finished until 1609–1610, because of "a lack of good means" and the revisers' "poor estate in banishment." Because it was eventually published in Douai, the entire Bible has been designated the Douai Version.

It is a translation from Jerome's Vulgate, which had been commended by St Augustine and declared authentic by the Council of Trent. As we have seen, the Roman Church considered the Vulgate to be the purest form of the original Bible. They believed that the Greek and Hebrew documents had been corrupted by the Jews and the early church. Some use of the Greek and Hebrew was made in the translation, but only slight traces of it can be found. According to the translators' own admission it was "translated . . . out of the authentic Latin, diligently conferred with the Hebrew, Greek, and other editions of divers languages." The use of the original languages was for the "discovery of the corruption of divers late translations." The Douai Version was thus a revision of the Latin Vulgate rather than a translation of the original languages.

The Douai Old Testament had fifty books, including eleven of the Apocrypha. In the Psalms, the translation was one further stage removed from the Hebrew original because Jerome had translated the Psalms from the Greek Septuagint version. The Psalms therefore had started in Hebrew, been translated into Greek, and from Greek into Latin, and now from Latin into English.

The notes were used to press Catholic interpretation and dogma against the "false and vain glosses of Calvin and his followers." Martin even went so far as to say that the English Bible was "not indeed God's book, worde, or Scripture, but the Devil's worde." But while the footnotes clash violently with those of the reformers, the translation does not differ greatly from the Protestant version. It was more literal, more Latinate, less easy for people with little education to understand, but it had some influence on the translators of the King James Version.

The jewel in the crown

On the death of Elizabeth, a childless queen, the reign of the Tudors came to an end. James VI of Scotland, the son of Mary Queen of Scots, became the next king of England. Unlike his mother, he was brought up with strong Protestant convictions, and a new day dawned for the puritan cause. Scotland, reformed by John Knox, was presbyterian to the core, so before he even arrived in London, James was met by a deputation which presented him with the "Millenary Petition." Signed by more than 800 puritan clergy, this petition requested the abolition of confirmation, an end to the sign of the cross in baptism and of the ring in

Hampton Court Palace, venue for the 1604 conference from which the King James' Version of the Bible sprang.

Opposite: **King James I of England; it is this King James whose name is immortalized in the "King James' Version."**

marriage, and the elimination of the terms "priest" and "absolution" in the Prayer Book. The petitioners assured the king, however, that they did not want to end the ecclesiastical state, merely reform it.

This led to a conference at Hampton Court in 1604, called by James to address the "things pretended to be amiss in the church." The first meeting was held on January 14, 1604, though the man who was thought to be the leader of the puritan group, Dr John Reynolds, had not been invited. Reynolds was an influential educator who has been described as the "third university of England." When he did meet with the conference members, on January 16, Reynolds argued, from the fact that the Bishops' Bible had ever been undertaken, that the Elizabethan bishops considered no translation (other than the Geneva version with its suspect notes) to be good enough for general use. The Great Bible was cumbersome, the Geneva spoiled by Calvinist notes, and the Bishops' of inferior quality. His logic was inescapable: either make the Geneva Bible the authorized version of England, or set about the task of creating a better translation.

The latter suggestion appealed to the king's vanity. On July 22, 1604, he announced that he had appointed fifty-four men to work on a new translation of the Bible under the guidance of Richard Bancroft, the Bishop of London, soon to become Archbishop of Canterbury. Bancroft was a high churchman, unsympathetic to puritan objectives, and it was nearly three years before the work started in earnest. By this time only forty-seven translators were named, but they represented the cream of England's intelligentsia.

Opposite: **Title page of the Authorized (King James') Version, 1611.**

A set of fourteen rules was drawn up for their guidance. The Bishops' Bible was to be followed with as few alterations as the Greek and Hebrew would permit. Other English translations were to be used only when they were more accurate. The chapter divisions were not to be altered, unless considered absolutely necessary. The old ecclesiastical terms were to be retained (such as "church", in preference to "congregation"). There were to be no marginal notes, except to explain a Hebrew or Greek word where the translation might be considered inadequate. (It is interesting to note that these marginal references numbered about 9,000 in the early editions, but later grew to over 60,000.)

The revisers included some scholars who were proficient in Hebrew, and some in Greek. They were divided into six committees, two meeting in Oxford, two in Cambridge and two in Westminster. Each committee was responsible for translating a section of the Bible. The sections were then sent to a select committee of twelve, composed of two scholars from each of the six committees. Lastly, two men, Thomas Bilson and Miles Smith, carried out final revision before the manuscript was sent to Robert Barker, the King's Printer.

The basis for the translation of the Old Testament was the Massoretic (Hebrew) text which had been printed in 1514–1517 in the Complutensian Polyglot. This was an edition which had Hebrew, Aramaic, Greek and Latin versions printed side by side. The translators also had a more recent polyglot, printed in Amsterdam in 1572, and other recent scholarly Latin translations. For the New Testament, they used the critical editions of the Greek text published in Geneva from 1550 onwards by Estienne and by Beza.

There are at least three reasons why this Bible should be considered the greatest translation up to that date. First, it was not the labor of one man, so it did not incorporate one man's weaknesses and blind spots; it was the effort of six committees, consisting of men who were the most learned scholars of their generation. Second, knowledge of Greek and Hebrew had greatly increased during the forty years which had elapsed since the last translation. Third, this was the age of Shakespeare, Spenser and Marlowe. The flowering of poetry and drama that took place during the Elizabethan age resulted in a Bible that was a masterpiece of English literature.

Unfortunately, typographical mistakes appeared in the first edition. In fact, there were two 1611 editions, with many hundreds of differences, and the 1613 edition differed from the edition of 1611 in as many as 400 places. All of this required numerous revisions, and led Dr John Lightfoot to encourage the House of Commons to consider "a review and survey of the translation of the Bible." It is reported that a committee for the British and Foreign Bible Society, examining six separate editions of the King James Bible, discovered nearly 24,000 variations in text and punctuation. A Cambridge Bible revision made in 1762 introduced 383

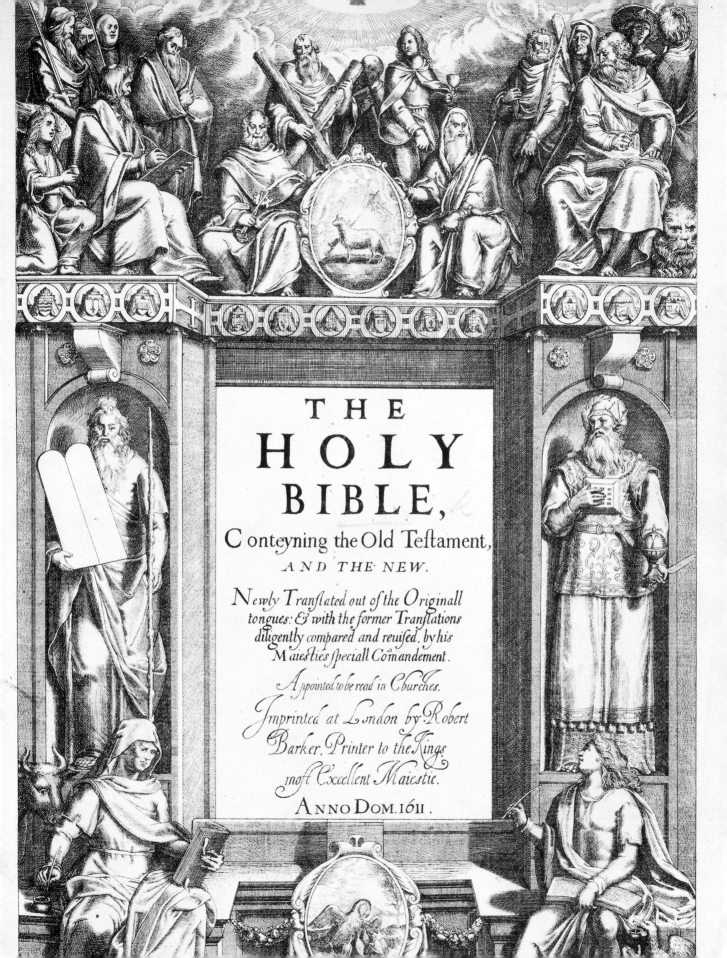

THE HOLY BIBLE,

C onteyning the Old Testament,
AND THE NEW.

Newly Translated out of the Originall
tongues: & with the former Translations
diligently compared and reuised, by his
Maiesties speciall Comandement.

Appointed to be read in Churches.

Imprinted at London by Robert
Barker, Printer to the Kings
most Excellent Maiestie.

ANNO DOM. 1611.

changes in the text and marginal notes; and a 1769 Oxford Bible introduced 76 changes in weights, measures and coins. These two editions are considered to be as nearly perfect in mechanical execution as human skill can make them.

The saga of Brewster

The village of Scrooby is about 146 miles north of London on the main road between London and Edinburgh. According to the Domesday Book, its manor house once belonged to the archbishops of York. In the reign of Elizabeth I this manor provided a stopping place for travelers, and a post office for the royal mail.

In the 1570s, the office of postmaster was held by a man named Brewster. His son, *William Brewster*, matriculated at Peterhouse, Cambridge, on December 3, 1580. Though we do not know what he studied there, we do know that he was converted to puritan doctrine.

In 1583 William Brewster was at home when William Davison arrived at the manor on the Queen's service. He stayed for an evening on his way to Edinburgh, his assignment, to frustrate the efforts of a French envoy who was trying to establish friendly relations between France and Scotland. Sixteen-year-old Brewster was so captivated by their conversation that he persuaded Davison to make him his assistant. The job took them overseas and introduced William Brewster to several important people; William Davison, in 1585, became secretary of state with Sir Francis Walsingham.

Brewster might have climbed the ladder in politics, had it not been for an incident in 1587. Queen Elizabeth had a death warrant for Mary Queen of Scots on her desk, awaiting her signature. She vacillated for a long time, but at last when Davison was present she quickly signed it and handed it to him, leaving him in charge of carrying it out. When she heard of Mary's execution, she called for the arrest of Davison, for "exceeding" her instructions. A jury fined him £6,666 (though his fine was subsequently remitted) and he was confined to the Tower for eighteen months. His collapse left William Brewster without a job, and he returned to Scrooby.

In the summer of 1590, when William was twenty-three, his father died, and after some controversy, William was appointed to assume his father's responsibilities.

That same year a child was born three miles away, whom his parents named *William Bradford*. Brewster was to have a lifelong friendship with William Bradford. In 1602, they started walking twelve miles to Gainsborough, to worship at the first separatist church in the north, which was meeting at the Old Hall. The church had just called John Smith, a Cambridge-educated man, to be their pastor.

Robert Browne was also educated at Cambridge before settling at

William Bradford, member of the Separatist church at Gainsborough.

Norwich. He strongly criticised the episcopal order, believing that the church should be separate and independent, accountable only to the local congregation. He became the founder of the Congregationalists. Though there was no link between Smith and Browne, the Gainsborough assembly was persecuted as "Brownists," and by 1606, Smith and several of his congregation were obliged to flee into exile. They escaped to Amsterdam, where Smith became a physician. After they had left, Brewster invited the remaining members of the church who still wished to meet, to use his manor. In the absence of a pastor, he became their spiritual adviser.

The Court House, Boston, where the would-be pilgrims were imprisoned.

John Robinson was a member of this new assembly. He had been minister of a congregation in Norwich, the birthplace of Brownism, and had had to flee from there for his own safety. This subjected the new assembly to further suspicion and persecution. Many members lost their property, paid heavy fines and suffered stiff prison sentences, without "any liberty or conference." It soon became apparent that they would have to go into exile if they were to retain their freedom of worship.

Emigration was difficult. A law dating from Richard II's time forbade emigration without a license, so passages abroad were clandestine and expensive. To compound the problem, a subpoena had been issued on September 15, 1607, for the apprehension of William Brewster. The authorities, however, were unable to locate him.

The group negotiated with a Dutch captain to meet them in the marshy waters near Fishtoft, outside Boston. They had loaded their goods and their families, and were waiting for the tide, when they were surrounded by catchpoles—sheriff's officials, usually responsible for tax collecting. The men were robbed, the women immodestly searched, and they were brought to the Guildhall in Boston. Seven of the leaders were imprisoned in two cells, and the records show that William Brewster "was the chief of those that were taken at Boston, and suffered the greatest loss."

Because the records are lost, we do not know how long the imprisonment lasted, or when they were liberated. Their next attempt to emigrate was in the early summer of 1608. This time a Dutch captain agreed to meet them at the mouth of the River Humber, sixty miles north of Boston. The women and children were to travel by boat while the men journeyed overland. The men were the first to arrive and were in the boat, waiting for the others, when the authorities came. The frightened captain immediately took off and headed for the open sea, leaving the women and children behind.

The authorities were frustrated, embarrassed, and sensitive to public opinion. They therefore allowed the women to go free, and by winter the families were united again in Amsterdam. This was the first stage in the harassing of the Puritans known as the Pilgrim Fathers.

Lands ho

The Pilgrims had surrendered their land and livings, and endured threats to their lives, all for the sake of liberty in worship. Joining a group who had emigrated to Amsterdam before them, they now numbered about a hundred. Amsterdam was an asylum for freedom fighters, but they nevertheless had a difficult time. All of them had left behind a farming life, but they were now forced to compete and survive in a world of trade and commercial transactions, an alien world to plain folk, who were utterly honest, hard working and conscientious to a fault.

Moreover, this readjustment in their lives had to be accomplished through a foreign language.

The Brewster group, under the spiritual leadership of John Robinson, stayed in Amsterdam for one year, and then moved to Leyden, about thirty-five miles to the south. There they lived an exemplary life for the next eleven years. Their numbers grew to about 300, the size of the church in Amsterdam. Their pastor became an honorable member of the university; their products were sought and used by other tradesmen, and any member of the church was given credit when it was needed. In fact, traveling English tradesmen such as Edward Winslow, Thomas Brewer, John Carver and Myles Standish cast their lot in with them, and even sailed the Atlantic to the new world in their company.

By 1620 it became obvious that they had to move once more. First, some were in financial difficulties. Second, their children were being conscripted into the Netherlands army, and some were submitting to the temptations of the city. Third, it was difficult to avoid assimilation into the Dutch community. Fourth, their safety was threatened by the war with Spain. Finally, they were threatened once more with persecution. William Brewster and Thomas Brewer had written books which had reached England, and James I wanted them brought before the courts.

They considered emigrating to Virginia—the leading merchant in the Virginia Company was a personal friend of Brewster's—but rejected this option because the company's charter enforced strict conformity to the Church of England. Absence from daily church service, for example, was punishable on the third offence by six months in the galleys, and

A canal in Leyden, the Netherlands. Brewster brought his group of English Separatists here before they emigrated to the New World.

A monument commemorating the sailing of the Mayflower; Boston, England.

the third absence from a Sunday service carried the death penalty. Loss of wages and whippings were common punishments for nonconformity.

Eventually the Pilgrims accepted a proposal from a group of seventy London merchants who had obtained a tract of land from the Plymouth Company, with the right to self-government for settlers. The shares in this company were sold for £10 each. The Pilgrims were to take their earnings after seven years, and divide them between the shareholders. A contingent from England were to join the Leyden group, and they were to cross the Atlantic in two vessels: a 60–ton pinnace called the *Speedwell*, and the 180–ton *Mayflower*, mastered by Thomas Jones. The *Speedwell* went to Holland to collect the Pilgrims, and bring them to Southampton before facing the Atlantic.

The journey to the new world began on August 5, 1620. There were thirty passengers on the *Speedwell* and ninety on the *Mayflower*. After battling against contrary winds for three days, the *Speedwell* sprang a leak, and had to pull into Dartmouth for repairs. There was a complete overhaul, and then they put to sea again. This time, 300 miles past Lands End, the *Speedwell* had another serious leak, and both ships returned to the closest port, Plymouth. Eighteen passengers became so frightened that they decided to stay behind, but the remaining 102 passengers crowded on to the *Mayflower* and took their chance.

Voyages across the Atlantic were exceedingly perilous. Of 180 men

The Pilgrim Fathers pray before setting sail from Delft, the Netherlands.

The Pilgrim Fathers land in America; first ashore were John Alden and Mary Chitton.

and women from the Amsterdam church who had set out for Virginia in March, 1619, only 50 survived the journey. Overcrowding and disease had taken the lives of the others—and this experience was common-place.

The first half of the journey was uneventful but then very strong gales began to batter their vessel. One of the main beams was twisted out of its place but one of the passengers had a power screw and, with his help, they were able to secure the beam. One storm followed another, but only one man's life was threatened. This man was John Howland, who had ventured above deck only to be immediately swept overboard. Miraculously, he managed to grab a coil of topsail halyards trailing in the water, and some sailors risked their lives to pull him back to safety. One of Samuel Fuller's servants died during the journey, and a baby was born. So the same number arrived as had left port in England.

On November 9, after nine weeks at sea, they sighted land, only to discover that it was outside the jurisdiction of the Plymouth Company. They were uncertain what to do, becuase there was no established authority there. Assuming that this meant freedom, the adult males gathered together and drafted the *Mayflower Compact.* It was signed by forty-one men, using the clothes chest belonging to William Brewster for a table. The *Mayflower Compact* stipulated that its signatories must leave the *Mayflower* group and settle elsewhere on their own.

Dying for a change

For two weeks the *Mayflower* sat outside the harbor, the longboat having been too severely battered by storms to be usable. A well-wooded coastline lay immediately in front of the Pilgrims, but rough seas prevented a landing. Eventually, on November 21 Myles Standish led the first expedition ashore. Myles was a soldier by profession, stationed in the Netherlands and had been employed by the Plymouth Company to protect their interests. He was attracted to these quiet and peaceable people but never became a member of their church and remained a Catholic. They landed on Cape Cod, now called Provincetown, and when they returned to the *Mayflower* they reported that apart from one brief encounter with some Indians, they were greatly encouraged.

The second expedition, on November 27, was led by Christopher Jones and they discovered the wreckage of a French fishing boat. The French proved to be their closest neighbors, 500 miles north in Nova Scotia. They found no suitable harbor, and no fresh water.

The third expedition set out on December 6, and took soundings in the harbor. On land they found cornfields and little running brooks. When this expedition returned to the *Mayflower*, William Bradford had

The Pilgrim Fathers give thanks after landing, in 1620.

sad news awaiting him. His wife, Dorothy May, had fallen overboard and drowned during his absence. The happy news was that the *Mayflower* was now able to sail into the harbor, and the long voyage had technically come to an end, twenty-seven days after their arrival.

On Monday, December 28, they finally decided on the exact location for the settlement, and that afternoon, twenty of them started building barricades. That evening, a tempest came that was so severe that the *Mayflower* had to drop all three of its anchors to stand the strain. After the storm, the men began to fell and carry timber. Their first job was to build a twenty-foot-square communal cabin. Then they divided the families into nineteen households, the single men being assigned to families so that they would need as few houses as possible. A street was plotted parallel to a stream. (Since 1823 it has been named Leyden Street.) The lots were then allocated.

Because of the delays caused by the *Speedwell* and the fierce storms on the Atlantic, the Pilgrims were unprepared for the severe winter. They had to convert their first house into a hospital, and disease raged so violently among them that there were scarcely enough people to care

Plymouth Rock, Plymouth, Massachusetts.

for those who were ill. Many died, sometimes two and three a day, mostly women, and were buried on Coles Hill. By the end of February, they had lost and buried thirty-one members of their group. Almost one half of all the Pilgrims were dead after the first two months.

By the middle of March, the sun was warm around noon and the birds were beginning to sing. Their first severe winter was over. Wolves would still howl at night and prowl by day, but it was not wolves the settlers dreaded so much as the Indians who were occasionally spotted. Myles Standish was authorized to organize a militia, and he brought the five cannons ashore from the *Mayflower*, stationing them on the Fort Hill platform, with a commanding view of every approach to the village. Then one morning, near the end of March, a startling event occurred.

The settlers were about to hold a meeting in their common house, when an Indian walked boldly down the middle of the street, and called out a resounding and hearty "Welcome!" in English. They prevented him from entering the common house until they found out who he was. He told them his name was Samoset, and he provided a rich harvest of information. He promised to bring an Indian called Squanto to meet them, and they both appeared on the following Thursday. Squanto was fluent in English. He was one of twenty-four Indians who had been kidnapped in 1614 by a pirate named Thomas Hunt and sold as slaves in Spain. Squanto had escaped and made his way to England, eventually working for the treasurer of the Newfoundland Company. When he had returned to the area he had discovered that he was the sole survivor of his tribe.

Squanto introduced the Pilgrims to an Indian chief by the name of Massasoit, who brought sixty of his braves with him. With great formality, Standish and Alterton, with six musketeers, approached a meeting point to face Massasoit and twenty of his armed warriors. The Indian chief had his face painted a dull red, and his warriors' faces were either red, black, yellow or white. The meeting was most amiable, with respectful salutes and gracious gestures, and a peace pact was organised between them that lasted for the next fifty years.

On April 5, 1621, the *Mayflower* hoisted her sails and set out once more for the open seas, breaking the last link that bound the Pilgrims to England. These courageous Pilgrims became the seeds of a new nation. They sacrificed fortunes and endured hardships solely for the freedom to worship God according to the dictates of their conscience. Prizing that liberty above life itself, they surmounted all obstacles to gain it.

In paying tribute to them, the forefathers of this great nation, we must also acknowledge the source of their inspiration, their comfort in sorrow, the magnet that drew them 3,000 miles across the cold and stormy Atlantic waters to a country beyond the edge of civilization. It was the book that for them was supreme in all matters of faith and practice—the "Indestructible Book."

Correcting the teacher

The next major undertaking in the work of Bible translation came some 275 years after the printing of the King James Version. The English language had changed, and independent scholars such as John Wesley in 1755 and Noah Webster in 1832 had produced their own revised translations of the whole Bible, or parts of it, reflecting those linguistic changes. Knowledge of the original languages had also developed. New manuscripts, such as the Sinaitic, Vatican and Alexandrian manuscripts, had been discovered, and textual criticism had become a science. In February 1870, Archbishop Wilberforce suggested to the Church of England's governing Convocations that there were sufficient reasons for a revision. The Convocation of York declined to be involved, admitting the blemishes in the King James Version but deploring "any recasting of the text." The Convocation of Canterbury, however, decided to proceed with the task.

John Wesley (1703–91).

A committee was formed of sixty-five members, of which fourteen either died or resigned. Thirty-six were Anglicans, and the rest were of various denominations, including one Unitarian. Cardinal Newman was invited to participate, but declined. It was Wilberforce's desire to involve Americans, and so the famous church historian Philip Schaff was asked to put together an American committee. In all, Schaff had thirty-four participating members, making an international total of ninety-nine members.

The work began in the Jerusalem Chamber of Westminster Abbey on June 22, 1870. The American committee began its work in the Bible House of New York City on October 4, 1872. A provisional revision of a small section was made in England, and sent to America for approval. The English then revised the draft on the basis of the Americans' comments, and sent the new draft back to America. Then England revised again to produce a more uniform style. The first revisions were approved by a simple majority of the committee; any subsequent revisions required a two-thirds vote. This meant that revisions were made at least five times, and sometimes seven revisions were required.

Though it had been intended that no alterations should be made to the Greek text used by the translators of the Authorized Version, exceptions were made when competent scholars believed that such changes were necessary. Therefore a new Greek text was constructed, known as the "Revisers' Text." Westcott and Hort's Greek text was published within five days of this revision of the Bible, and they had both served on the revision committee, but the Revisers' Text differed from Westcott and Hort in about 200 places, and from the text used by the King James translators in 5,788 readings.

This version was called the English Revised Version, and it is said that it has 36,191 changes. If anyone were to ask whether it had any value, the answer would definitely be yes. First, archaic and unintelligible words were replaced. The word "let," for example, meant "hinder" in 1611, but today means "permit." The word "prevent" came from the Latin *pre venio*, to "go before" or "precede," and did not have today's meaning of "stop."

Second, the revisers aimed at consistency in translation. They wanted each Greek or Hebrew word to be translated by the same English word every time it appeared. The Greek word "meno," for example, is used 117 times in the Greek text, but is translated by ten different English words in the King James Version. The Greek word "dunamis" means "power," but is translated by thirteen different English words in the King James Version. On the other hand, in the King James Version the single English word "power" translates seventeen different Hebrew words in the Old Testament, and six Greek words in the New Testament.

Third, the old chapter and verse divisions were relegated to the margin, while the content was divided into paragraphs. The former aids you in finding the material, while the latter aids you in finding the message.

Fourth, where Greek grammar differs from English grammar, the revisers tried to give an accurate rendering of the Greek. (Greek, for example, has fewer tenses than English, and has no indefinite article.) As a result, however, the Revised Version suffered from excessive literalism.

The Revised Version was a phenomenal success when the first copies of the New Testament came off the presses on May 17, 1881. Oxford and Cambridge presses each had a million advance orders. On May 20 the first shipment arrived in the United States. It was due to be on sale in the shops on May 21, but copies were immediately being sold on the streets of New York and Philadelphia. On May 20 alone New York sold 365,000 copies, and Philadelphia over 110,000 copies. Chicago was 978 miles away, and the *Tribune* and the *Times* did not wish to wait until more New Testaments could be shipped over. They employed ninety-two compositors and five correctors to wire Matthew through Romans, that is 118,000 words. This was the longest message ever sent over the wires. The task was accomplished in twelve hours and the text appeared in newspapers on May 22, 1881. It was estimated that three million copies were sold in England and America within one year of publication. Without dispute, no book can compare to this "Indestructible Book."

Straining the gnat

The American attitude to the Revised Version was slightly negative. All final decisions on translation had been made in England, and some preferences which the Americans had expressed were rejected by the English committee. To offset this, the English proposed that the American preferences should be published in an appendix, and appear in every copy of the Revised Version for the next fourteen years. By that time, the Americans expected that scholars, and the general public, would approve the American preferences. As part of the agreement, the American company agreed not to sanction any revised Bibles other than those published by Oxford and Cambridge university presses. This tied the hands of the American committee from 1885 to 1899.

The English committee disbanded after their translation was finished, and the publishers indicated that they had no intention of incorporating the American preferences in any future publications. So the American company did *not* disband. Under pressure from the public, certain publishers issued unauthorized editions of the New Testament incorporating the American preferences listed in the appendix, and Oxford and Cambridge published an "American Revised version" of the whole Bible in 1898. But the American committee wanted all their preferred readings incorporated, and not just those which had been selected for inclusion in the published appendix. When the fourteen years of the agreement had expired and they were no longer hampered by the English committee and publishers, they produced their own revision. It was published in 1901 and became known as the American Standard Revised version.

Most of the differences between the English and American versions seem small, but many scholars consider them to be decided improvements. For example, the Americans used shorter paragraphs than the English, and put blank spaces between the main divisions, especially in the epistles. Verse divisions were placed in the text, instead of—as previously—in the margin.

There were also many changes in translation. For example, the words "Holy Spirit" replaced all references to the "Holy Ghost." The plural "devils" was not used, since there is only one "devil," but many "demons" (subordinate to the devil). The word "covenant" was consistently used in place of the word "testament."

There was also an attempt to drop archaic forms and spellings, such as "holpen" for "helped," "hale" for "drag away," and "wot" or "wist" for "know." American words were substituted for English words. For example, the word "grain" was used instead of "corn" because, though in England the word "corn" implied grain of all kinds, in America it suggested maize, or Indian corn. The word "platter" was used instead of "charger," which in America meant a horse.

The reception was as expected: the American Standard Version dominated the American market, and the Revised Version the English market. The ASV was widely considered to be the more accurate, and some pulpits and seminaries began using only the ASV.

Another offspring of the King James Version came in 1979 when Nelson published the New King James Bible. This was an attempt to "maintain the lyrical quality" and "majesty of the form" of the 1611 version.

Even where they felt it necessary to introduce a new translation, the revisers made an effort to maintain "the general vocabulary of the 1611 version." They modernized the pronouns, eliminated archaic verb endings, and made minor changes in other grammatical forms.

Nelson also introduced several new features. The paragraphs were given headings, to enable the reader to identify the subject matter. The poetic sections were printed in contemporary verse forms to suggest the beauty of the original passage. Old Testament quotations were printed in oblique type, and footnotes indicated the Old Testament reference. Also, some of the italicized words, used by the translators of the King James Version to give clarity beyond the literal translation, were eliminated in the New King James Version.

The most important difference between this and all other modern translations of the scripture arises from the text from which the work was translated. The traditional Greek text underlying the 1611 edition was replaced by the "neutral text" of Westcott and Hort. That textual base eliminated many words, phrases and verses used by the translators of the King James Version. While there is heated controversy on this issue today, it was maintained by the scholars preparing the New King James Version that "the nineteenth-century text suffers from over-revision, and the traditional Greek text is more reliable than previously supposed."

So many versions

As we have seen, the Bible was first written in Hebrew, Aramaic and Greek. Pope Damasus had it translated into Latin but his successors would not allow it to be made accessible to other nations and later generations. To read the Bible, people had to learn Latin—and even then the Bible's circulation was often restricted to the priesthood.

The Reformation came to England because scholars started learning Greek, the language of the New Testament. They knew the Bible would have the same impact on anyone who could read it—so they translated the Bible into English. And they were right: England was rocked by the Reformation.

A few statistics

Even before Wycliffe there were about forty translations into Old and Middle English, admittedly only covering sections of the Bible, mostly the Psalms. From the time of Wycliffe's Bible, hand-written and translated into Middle English about 1380, until the time of the next major English translation, that of Tyndale in 1525, there were another twenty-six translations, including Wycliffe's Bible and its several revisions. From 1525 to the publication of the King James Version in 1611 there were some 212 editions of the Bible, complete or in part. That makes a grand total of 277 separate efforts to translate the Bible into the language of the English-speaking people.

Between the publication of the King James Version in 1611 and the American Standard Version in 1901, there were no less than 522 attempts by translators, revisers or editors to discover the exact meaning of the original text of the Bible and express it precisely in current English. That makes about 800 attempts to overcome linguistic barriers, and communicate the message of the Bible.

Statistics are not available beyond 1985, but between 1901 and 1985 no less than 440 efforts were recorded. From the time when the English language was in its early stages until 1985, the grand total of translations, improved editions or independent paraphrases comes to about 1,240.

Roman Catholic translations

There had already been a Roman Catholic Bible Society in existence for over fifty years when, in the mid-nineteenth century, Pope Pius IX warned against the distribution of scriptures without any guidance in their interpretation! That society published the Rheims-Douai version without notes, leaving the reader to make his own interpretation. It also produced several other translations of the Bible into English. Between 1811 and 1816 they produced five editions of the Bible and two of the New Testament. There have also been several Catholic translations in the twentieth century, the most wellknown being the Jerusalem Bible of 1966, which was translated directly from the Hebrew, Greek or Aramaic. In 1985 this was extensively revised as the New Jerusalem Bible.

Translations by Jews

We must not forget the English Bible produced by the Jews. For the Jews the Middle Ages were not conducive to the sort of scholarship required for Bible translation, but by the year 1400, translations of the Jewish Bible began to appear in various languages. In 1789, the year of the French Revolution, a version of the Pentateuch appeared, claiming to be derived from the King James Version. In 1853, a Hebrew Bible came out that became the favorite of English and American synagogues. The Jewish Publication Society decided to revise that work, and it was published in 1917. Several different versions appeared in the 1960s and 70s, and in 1985 the three largest branches of organized Judaism in America produced a monumental work of scholarship entitled the *TaNaKh*, a new translation of what Christians call the Old Testament.

A book for the world

Because we are considering the impact of one book on the whole human race, it is not fair to limit our survey to one language. The Hebrew was translated in to Greek, and later into Latin, and both those translations fathered many others. The first printed German Bible dates back to 1466,

Opposite: Queen Victoria presents a Bible in the Audience Chamber at Windsor; painting by Thomas Jones Barker, 1861.

and eighteen other editions were printed before Luther gave the Germans his Bible. John Calvin revised his first French Bible as late as 1551. The Dutch had several versions by both Catholics and Protestants; in 1537 they were given a version based on the original texts, and this was revised as late as 1897. The Italians also had several versions, legal and illegal; and the Spanish, who prohibited a vernacular Bible in the first printed Index of the Spanish Inquisition, were given a literal interpretation in 1553, presented by a Jewish organization.

In Europe, complete or partial Bibles have appeared in Czech, Danish, Hungarian, Icelandic, Norwegian, Polish, Portuguese, Russian, Swedish and other languages. And after William Carey arrived in India in 1793, and before 1834, there were translations of Scripture into more than 34 far Eastern languages. In fact, the British and Foreign Bible Society listed 10,000 versions in 628 languages between the year 1400 and the early 1900s.

People in many countries and through many centuries have displayed a passion for translating the Bible. They have willingly paid the cost, even when that cost had meant giving up their lives, in order to break down the linguistic barriers between men and women and this Indestructible Book.

Printer's ink

When Bibles were first published in England it was the policy to use only the Oxford and Cambridge university presses and the King's Printers. (Since before Henry VII's death, there had been an official "King's Printer.") Later on, however, translations of the Bible, and translations into other languages, were not so restricted. And, of course, we know from the story of the Tyndale and Coverdale versions that publishers were always printing unauthorized Bibles.

British and Foreign Bible Society

Nearly two hundred years ago, a nonconformist minister named Thomas Charles was preaching in Bala in Wales. During the service, he asked a young girl to repeat the text of the previous Sunday's sermon. She cried, and explained that the weather was so bad that she had been unable to check the Welsh Bible. Charles found out that the closest Welsh Bible was seven miles away from her home. That incident so impressed him that he went to London to ask for help and this led to the founding of the British and Foreign Bible Society in 1804. By 1928, the Society had circulated over 385 million Bibles, with versions in 608 languages. They had 5,142 auxiliary branches in England and Wales, plus another 5,000 overseas, and they employed 900 book agents to sell Bibles from door to door, because it was against their policy to give any away free.

During 1930 alone, the British and Foreign Bible Society published

A Bible Society Bible-van at a market in Zaïre.

12 million copies of the Bible, in 643 languages. They were shipped to every corner of the world in 4,583 boxes, weighing 490 tons. And that is but one Bible Society, in one country, in one year.

Voltaire, the noted French infidel, predicted that within a hundred years Christianity would be swept off the earth and the Bible would be found only in museums. The British and Foreign Bible Society later bought his Paris house as a depot for the distribution of Bibles.

United Bible Societies

While there are Bible societies which operate independently, such as Britain's Trinitarian Bible Society, there are 110 national Bible societies worldwide, including the British and Foreign Bible Society and the American Bible Society, which operate under the umbrella of the United Bible Societies. In 1990 the American Bible Society distributed over six million Bibles, New Testaments or portions (a portion usually means at least one of the sixty-six books of the Bible) in the United States alone. Nearly 14.4 million more were distributed overseas, making over 20.4 million altogether. They used over 60,000 volunteers operating out of more than 1,300 centers.

The United Bible Societies provide an ecumenical Bible, in ordinary everyday language, and are placing copies in the hands of millions of people around the world who would otherwise have no access to a Bible. Their aim is to tackle the language barriers and provide translations wherever there are more than a million people. China may be a good example. When it was reported that in some areas 90,000 people were sharing twenty-five Bibles between them, the United Bible Society provided them with printing facilities, within China, to the value of over $5 million. This one printing facility gave the Chinese an additional capacity for 250,000 Bibles and 500,000 New Testaments every year. According to their January 1987 report, United Bible Societies also provided the paper for printing 300,000 copies of a new Chinese translation of the Gospels.

Getting the Bible out
The three leading Bible publishers in the year 1932 were the British and Foreign Bible Society, the American Bible Society and the National Bible Society of Scotland. Together they produced 22,626,867 complete Bibles, New Testaments and scripture portions in many different tongues. If those Bibles had been stacked one on top of another, they would have reached twenty-eight miles above the earth's surface—five times the height of Mount Everest.

Today, there are 6,170 separate languages on earth, according to the Wycliffe Bible Translators, and at least one book of the Bible has been translated into 1,978 of these languages. Some of these Bibles are printed from left to right, others from right to left, and still others from top to bottom. There are some tribes who will not read anything printed, only what is written. So their Bible is first written, then photographed and copied on the presses. One Bible has thirty-nine volumes, because it is in Braille. Some of the languages and alphabets are so different from ours that they challenge the most skilled linguists. While the Russian alphabet has thirty-six letters, Tamil has 400 and Maori only fourteen. But none of these obstacles has dampened the zeal of translators or printers.

Many organizations are dedicated to distributing Bibles free of charge; the largest is probably the Gideons. Their estimated distribution for the year 1992 was 35 million. They have been producing Bibles for so long that in 1990 they were able to give the 500 millionth to President George Bush. The remarkable feature of this ministry is that every Bible is personally presented, through a staff of a little over 183,000 volunteers, all organized by only fifty-four paid employees.

It is estimated that over 44 million Bibles are sold every year, and another 35 million distributed free. This totals nearly 80 million every year. No other book has ever matched the popularity of this "Indestructible Book."

The sap is in the tree

It is not an exaggeration to say that the Bible has become part of the warp and woof of American society. If you doubt this, look at the people who have been influenced by the Bible, and its effects on our society.

Opposite: David Livingstone, Scots explorers, died in Africa, having just finished reading his Bible.

Mastered by the Bible

Nearly every branch of knowledge and every sphere of human endeavor has had its masters who have submitted to the supremacy of this book. David Livingstone, the great explorer, died kneeling at a cot in the heart of Africa. He had just finished reading his Bible.

Napoleon Bonaparte once commented to three generals who were in his room: "That Bible on the table is a book to you; it speaks to me; it is as it were a person."

When he was on his death bed, Scotland's great literary giant, Sir Walter Scott, asked his friend Lockhart to read to him from the book. Scott had a library of 20,000 volumes, so Lockhart asked him, "What book would you like?" Scott replied: "Need you ask? There is but one."

George Müller, the builder of the huge orphanage in Bristol, said: "I have read the Bible through one hundred times and found something new and inspiring every time."

England's King George V, as he promised his mother, read his Bible every day.

William Gladstone, four times Prime Minister of Great Britain, wrote a book which he entitled *The Impregnable Rock of Holy Scripture.* He professed to know ninety-five great men in the world of his day, and eighty-seven of them, he said, "were followers of the Bible."

Men who publicly professed allegiance to the Bible and served as President of the United States include George Washington, Thomas Jefferson, Abraham Lincoln and Franklin Roosevelt. The Bible is in every court-room. Every hospital is a monument to its moral influence.

Turn the coin over and look at the subject from the other side. Take the Bible out of literature, and what is left? Tennyson used over 300 quotations from the pages of the Bible. It has been calculated that Shakespeare has over 500 ideas and phrases taken directly from the pages of the Bible. Charles Dickens said: "It is the best book that ever was or ever will be in the world."

Or look at its contribution to the world of music. Take the Bible from Bach, Handel and Mozart, and what is left? Would we have ever heard of Handel, had it not been for his Bible? Look at the world of art. Where would the names of Leonardo da Vinci, Michelangelo, Donatello, Rembrandt, and Raphael be found, it they had not been inspired by the themes of the Bible?

Look back to the early days of many educational institutions and you will see they are inseparably linked with the church. Harvard, Yale, William and Mary and Dartmouth were all founded for the express purpose of training religious ministers. Dr. William Phelps, once Principal of Yale University, the third oldest educational institution in the United States, is quoted as saying: "I believe that a knowledge of the Bible without a college course is more valuable than a college course without a knowledge of the Bible."

Oliver Cromwell's statue outside the Palace of Westminster shows him clasping his sword in one hand, his Bible in the other.

Opposite: John Bunyan, the tinker who wrote *The Pilgrim's Progress*, and whose English style is imbued with the English Bible.

Dynamite

Then look at the effect the Bible has had. Consider John Adams, for example, who was a member of the mutinous crew of the Bounty. When the mutineers on Pitcairn Island died of syphilis, leaving Adams with all the women and children, he found his comfort and guidance in an old Bible he had found among the debris of the wrecked ship. By the time the American ship, the Topaz, discovered them, their jail was empty, and the church was geographically and spiritually in the center of their life. Is the relationship between the reform and the Bible merely coincidental?

John Gifford was among a small detachment of Cavaliers cornered by Oliver Cromwell's army and offered "surrender, or no quarter." Only Gifford was captured alive; the rest were killed. As he was waiting for his execution, his sister managed to distract the guard long enough to enable him to escape. He ran and hid in Bedford, where his profligate life and drunken debaucheries made him infamous. Eventually, someone introduced him to a Bible. The change was so radical that he became the minister of St John's Church in the same town. In fact, he was the original of Mr Interpreter in Bunyan's *Pilgrim's Progress*.

George Whitefield made Englishmen and Americans confront the issues of the Bible in what was then a novel way: he took the Bible out of the church and, by open air preaching, gave it in the country. As many as 30,000 to 60,000 would crowd together in the open to listen to his sermons. Thousands were transformed by their exposure to his Bible messages. Even Benjamin Franklin admired Whitefield and his work.

It was the Bible that influenced John Howard and Elizabeth Fry. In obedience to its teachings they created the public pressure which forced Parliament to reform the prison system. It was the Bible that led William Wilberforce to crusade for the emancipation of slaves. It was the Bible that motivated William Booth to build an army to help the destitute and homeless. It was the Bible that consoled Sir Ernest Shackleton in his lonely and hazardous experience of exploring Antarctica. And that same Bible influenced Sir James Young Simpson, who took the savagery out of surgery when he discovered chloroform. Simpson told an audience that the Bible was his greatest discovery.

There can be little dispute that the "Indestructible Book" has changed the world.

Look back over your shoulder

And so the story is told. It is the phenomenal story of a book that began with one man trying to care for a small nation travelling in a wilderness, and wanting to provide them with a moral code by which to regulate their lives. Historians and priests took up the story, wise men, poets, and prophets completed the message. Their writings were collected

together in twenty-two books—our Old Testament. At Jamnia, in AD 100, a rabbinical gathering settled any dispute for the Jewish nation by claiming that those books were the "Torah," or God's revelation to mankind.

After 400 years without any prophetic voice, the man whom some called the Christ (meaning "the Anointed," or Messiah) selected twelve unlikely men to be his apostles. They were unlikely to succeed as a team, for they were so diverse, including among their number a traitor and an underground fighter. Even less did it seem likely that they would contribute to the sacred book, being "unlearned and ignorant men" (Acts 4:13). Yet because of their words twenty-seven more books were added to the list. In AD 397 these books were officially approved as the complete canon of Scripture.

The Jewish nation did not accept the last twenty-seven books, so the Christian church became caretaker of this unique volume. Waves of persecution broke out against the church, leaving it bloody but unbroken; in fact, it grew in strength during each onslaught. In AD 303 the Emperor Diocletian ordered the destruction of every building used for a church, and every copy of the Bible that could be found. He even built an arch to commemorate the erasing of Christianity. But fifty years later, the succeeding emperor ordered the reproduction of fifty Bibles, at the government's expense. The church rose, singing a song of victory.

Persecution gave way to materialism. The Emperor Constantine joined the ranks of the believers. His governmental policies became the government of the church; his standard of living became the life style of its clergy; and his dependence on ritual became a passion in the church. Slowly the church deteriorated until the authority of tradition took the place of the book. Lust, greed, immorality and secularism came to the fore; the Bible was hidden away, buried in a foreign language.

But a light emerged in the dark night sky, "the morning star of the Reformation." John Wycliffe was a man with a brilliant mind, a tender conscience and a backbone of steel. He challenged the decadence of his day and, when necessary, defied the pope and his church, the king and his barons, and all the university professors of England. He gave to a small army of preachers a passion that burned like fire. His supreme undertaking was to inspire men to crack the Latin shell of the Bible and reclothe the message in the language of Middle English, bringing it out of the convent and scattering it throughout the country. Some 135 years later reformers were breaking down the flood dams all over Europe.

When the humanist scholar Erasmus published the first accessible New Testament in Greek, a new life force was experienced among Greek scholars. Men and women saw the impact that the Bible would have in the vernacular. Bibles started appearing in German, in French and in English. While in Germany it was the reform which produced the Bible, in England it was the Bible that produced the reform. Different translations in English became associated with the names of Tyndale,

Coverdale and Rogers; and then committees produced the Geneva Bible, the Bishops' Bible and finally—the cream of such efforts—the Authorized Version of King James I.

While the reformed Church of England kept the structural form of the Roman Catholic Church, Puritans drifted to the periphery of the church, and eventually some broke away. The splinters became the seeds of Protestant denominations, and persecution led some to migrate to lands where freedom of religion might be tolerated. So William Brewster's group came to Plymouth Rock. What they were to this nation, the Geneva Bible was to them. It was supremely important, vital beyond measure and authoritative in every matter of faith and practice. Those Pilgrim Fathers meticulously planted this book, like seeds, in the minds of their offspring. It provided the moral fiber for that early society. Religious meetings took priority over commercial pursuits, and violation of the sabbath was a punishable offense.

Christopher Columbus claimed that his voyage which discovered America was born while he was reading Isaiah. The Liberty Bell bears an inscription from Leviticus 25:10. Every single charter of the fifty states is written in words and concepts taken from the Bible.

Of the ten earliest colleges in America, nine were founded by the churches, and the other by the evangelist George Whitefield.

During the Civil War, the American Bible Society printed 7,000 Bibles daily for each side in the dispute. In 1864, the Memphis Bible Society sent a shipment of cotton to New York in return for 50,000 portions of scripture.

Today, the Bible is present at the inauguration of every President, and it is in the courts for the swearing in of every witness. Its sales have doubled since 1960. In 1991, 44 million copies were sold. Why? In the Old Testament, the volume is referred to as "the Word of God," 3,808 times.

Index